SERVICE TO COUNTRY - SOUTH DAKOTA STYLE

BY: LEE T. RAINES

Copyright © 2022 by Lee Raines

All rights reserved.

About the Author:

Though he has lived in Texas since the late 1980s, Lee Raines considers his early years in Groton, SD, as formative and influential on his values and success today. He was born in Britton, SD, in 1953, grew up in Groton, graduating from Groton High School in 1971. He served in the US Army from December 1972 to May 1976, and graduated from University of South Dakota in May 1978, attending college on the GI Bill. For the past 25 years, he has worked for Leif Johnson Ford in Austin, TX, in capacities that include manager of a dealership, chief financial officer and director of special projects. He lives with his partner, Julie Jerome and their dog Izzy in Austin, TX.

TABLE OF CONTENTS:

VETERANS – FROM WWII THROUGH
    VIETNAM ERA 1

DOUGLAS HEGDAHL – THE INCREDIBLY
    STUPID ONE 51

WWII – KOREA FROM 1940 THROUGH 1955 59

1956 THROUGH 1961 139

US ARMY IN THE 1960s AND EARLY 1970s 167

Veterans— From WWII through Vietnam Era

While growing up in Groton, my recollection of veterans was limited to watching a few men marching down the main street during parades, carrying flags, and wearing uniforms that did not seem to fit. My father and his friends never seemed to discuss their military experiences. I look back on those days and wonder if the war conversations took place in quiet places or over beers at the American Legion away from the family or away from people who did not serve. Until I started on this book, I had no idea how many veterans we had or what they had accomplished. I wish I knew then what I know now and would have been able to say thank you. I really took the "greatest generation" for granted. I wish I was given the opportunity to listen to their stories.

I start this discussion by talking about The Wall (the Vietnam conflict memorial in Washington DC), Vietnam, and the men who were killed in combat in our area. On to individuals who served during that period but did not serve in Vietnam. Followed by the individuals who served during WWII and the Korean War, then the period between 1956-1961. The number of veterans from our area is incredibly high, considering the number of available young men to serve. One might conclude that our area was filled with young men hell-bent on serving their country like their fathers. Or more likely, it could also be concluded that the impact of economics left no alternatives available to farm boys or those from small towns with limited opportunities. Farms during this period were small, crop yields were low, and farmers simply went from year to year hoping their banker could assist when needed. The sons and daughters graduated from high school, but college was typically out of the question. Since the farms needed fewer and fewer men to operate them, sons, and in some cases, daughters, needed to fend for themselves. The military ended up being one of those alternatives, at least in the short-term. Like their fathers, many of these individuals choosing to serve did so with the idea of using the GI Bill to finance an education, buy and finance a house, or give them a chance to see the world outside of South Dakota.

Each of the individuals who served either enlisted or were drafted. The drafts generally enabled certain individuals to avoid military service by attending college, teaching, age restrictions, physical abilities, etc. However, the young men from our area had limited options. As a result, they were called by their country, and they served without complaint.

All the individuals listed were either raised in the area or called the area their home. Veterans are included here from the areas surrounding Groton, Andover, Columbia, Verdon, Ferney, Claremont, and Hecla, to name just a few little towns. The largest town, Groton, had only 600 residents in the early 1960s, and the other little towns had less than 300 residents. The number of students who graduated from high school from this entire area probably did not exceed 120 each year, and with only half of them being boys, only 60 or so men became eligible for service each year. The military penetration was always very high, and this continued well into the early 1970s.

More Than a Name on The Wall

There was a song written by Jimmy Fortune and John Malanghton V. Remmel some years ago and made popular by The Statler Brothers. It memorialized the thoughts of a mother when she first saw the Wall in Washington DC. *More Than a Name on The Wall* commemorates the fallen soldiers of the Vietnam conflict/war or whatever term you would like to use to discuss the fiasco the US and other countries went through in their attempt to stop communism in the Far East. Little did we know that the cost of communism itself would be its undoing later. No one needed to fight to stop it. Just another government approach that would fail. What started out as a minor "saving Vietnam from the communists" became a wrenching, tearing-apart-our-country war and eventually resulted in the death of over 59,000 young men. The Wall lists every person lost and is visited by thousands of people each year. Everyone associated with the Vietnam generation should or has seen it, and no one can visit it and not be moved. I have seen it many times, and each time, I stop to look at the name I most associate with the Vietnam conflict, that being a man I did not really know. I just went to school with his brothers. That person is:

William Ernest Pasch, US Army, Specialist 4, born October 3, 1947, and died May 11, 1968, was from Groton, South Dakota. Pasch graduated from Groton High School in 1965. He was born into a family of relatively economically, disadvantaged farmers and was survived by his parents and three brothers. One was Alroy, who graduated with me in 1971 and another brother, Bob who graduated in

William Pasch

1970. A younger brother, Donnie was seven or eight years younger. Alroy passed away in 1983, but Bob is still kicking around Groton. Not sure what happened to Donnie. Pasch was a member of M Company, 3rd Squadron, of the 11th Armored Cavalry Regiment. Otherwise known as the 11th ACR. Pasch was a tank or assistant tank commander. He was killed when a rocket or mortar hit his tank, probably killing him and his crew instantly. Pasch died in a place that is not widely known, called Binh Duong Province, South Vietnam. He was 20 years old. We lost a young man, cut down in his early years of life. Another loss among 59,000. Pasch was awarded the Purple Heart, the Combat Infantry Badge, the Military Merit Medal, and the Gallantry Cross with Palm. His mother said at the funeral, "We have buried him with honors that are due for a brave soldier. His grave we decked with flowers and the flag he helped to save. He is gone but not forgotten." Another casualty of the conflict. Pasch is commemorated at Panel 58E, Line 24, of the Wall. Pasch had been in-country less than four months when he was killed.

Let me write the words to the song and let them roll around in your brain a while.

More Than a Name on a Wall

I saw her from a distance, as she walked up to the wall.

In her hand she held some flowers, as her tears began to fall.

She took out pen and paper as to trace her memories.

She looked up to heaven and the words she said were these.

She said, "Lord my boy was special, and he meant so much to me.

And oh, I'd love to see him just one more time, you see.

All I have are the memories and the moments to recall.

So, Lord could you tell him he's more than a name on the wall."

She said, "He really missed the family, being home on Christmas Day.

And he died for God and country in a place so far away.

I remember just a little boy, playing war since he was three.

And, Lord, this time I know, he's not coming home to me."

She said "Lord, my boy was special, and he meant so much to me.

And oh, I'd love to see him, but I know it just can't be.

So, I thank you for my memories and the moment to recall.

But Lord could you tell him he's more than a name of the wall.

Lord could you tell him he's more than a name on the wall."

There are differing numbers as to how many South Dakota men died in Vietnam. I have seen statistics that vary from 192 to slightly more than 200. The first person from South Dakota to die in Vietnam was Alvin Adam Leota from Leola. He died April 21, 1964. The last person to die in Vietnam from South Dakota was Howard Elmer Drain from Custer. He died March 17, 1972.

During these eight years, 13 young men from Brown County were lost, five from Day County and Marshall County lost two. I hope you do not mind, but I would like to list a few of those lost from our area (Andover, Groton, Columbia, Turton, Milbank, Pierpont, and Webster). Growing up in the 1960s, it is possible that each of us may have crossed their paths either from a school activity or in our day-to-day lives. What is provided is based upon public information. I chose not to make personal contact with survivors or friends and simply respect their privacy.

1. **Roger Sletten Cameron**, US Army, Warrant Officer (Helicopter Pilot), 334th Assault Helicopter Company, 145th Aviation Battalion, 12th Aviation Group, 1st Aviation Brigade. Born October 10, 1944, died January 31, 1968. Cameron died when his helicopter was shot down. He died in Dinh Tuong Province, South Vietnam. Cameron was born and raised in Pierpont and assigned to Vietnam in May 1967 and died January 31, 1968. Services were held in the Pierpont High School auditorium in early March 1968, and he was buried in the Pierpont Cemetery. He was survived by his parents and two brothers. When he died, he must have been "short," meaning his time left in Vietnam was coming to an end. Cameron was the Pierpont High School carnival king (along with the queen—Eunice Wenschlag) in 1961 and a member of the Pierpont basketball team. During the 1962 basketball season, Cameron was a starting member of the team averaging 20-plus points per game. He appeared to always be an integral part of the team in 1961 and 1962. Cameron graduated from Pierpont in 1962 and

Roger Sletten Cameron

worked for the Cameron Construction Company (likely a family business) until he entered the service in August 1965. In February 1968, he was reported by the military as missing in action and sometime during the week of February 19, 1968, he was declared killed in action. Cameron is commemorated on the Wall at Panel 36E, Line 1.

2. **Ronald Clifford Dexter**, US Marine, Private First Class, Company D., 1st Battalion, 26th Marines, 3rd MARDIV, III MAF. Dexter was born in Graceville, Minnesota, in 1947 and lived in Milbank where he graduated from high school in 1965. While in the marines, Dexter was married and shortly there-
Roland Dexter

after, July 9, 1966, left for Vietnam. Dexter died from small arms fire on September 19, 1966. He was survived by his wife, daughter, two brothers, a sister, and his parents. He was killed in Quang Tri Province, South Vietnam. He had been in-country only about two months. Dexter is commemorated on the Wall at Panel 10E, Line 117.

3. **Lanny Ray Krage,** US Marine, Lance Corporal, Company F., 2nd Battalion, 1st Marines, 1st MARDIV, III MAF. Krage was born in Aberdeen in January 1947 and died in the Quang Nam Province, South Vietnam. Krage graduated from Columbia High School in 1965. In the fall of 1965, Krage entered
Lanny Ray Krage

South Dakota State College. Krage was an integral part of the Columbia basketball and football teams while in high school. At graduation, Krage was six feet, four inches tall and weighed 230 pounds. Very large farm boy back in the day. On one occasion in December 1964, he scored 40 points against Bath and 33 against Veblen in January 1965. He was always one of the top scorers on the basketball team. He was a member of the Columbia basketball team that went to the State B in 1962. On the football field (eight-man), Krage excelled as a defensive lineman and as a large imposing running back on offense. In 1964, he was named to the All Prairie Team as a defensive end and running back. He was also on the All Prairie Team as an offensive guard in 1963. After enrolling in South Dakota State, Krage tried out for the football team and was an offensive tackle for the Jackrabbit Frosh Football Team. At the end of the first semester (December 1965), Krage enlisted in the marines. He graduated from basic training in June 1966. On October 20, 1966, Krage left for Vietnam, and he died on April 21, 1967. He had been in country for approximately six months. Krage was survived by his parents and one brother, Wayne, who graduated from Groton High School in 1968. Krage is commemorated on the Wall at Panel 18E, Line 61.

4. **Bernhardt W. (Pee Wee) Miller,** US Army, Private First Class, C Company, 3rd Battalion, 12th Infantry, 4th Infantry Division, USARV. His home of record was Shelby, Montana. He was born in 1942 and died November 10, 1967. He was a ground casualty from multiple fragmentation wounds. He died in Kontun

Province, South Vietnam. He was survived by his parents, two brothers, and three sisters. Pee Wee was born in Bowdle, South Dakota. He started his tour of duty in South Vietnam in late August 1967 and died less than three months later. In February 1968, word was received that Miller had been awarded the Bronze Star with Valor for attempting to aid an injured comrade and being killed. The bronze star was presented to his parents by Major M.A. Andersen of Webster. The reason I am including him in this discussion is because he lived in Groton for 10 years prior to his death. I found little information about Pee Wee from the Aberdeen or Groton papers and could find no indications that he graduated from Groton High School. Miller is commemorated on the Wall at Panel 29E, Line 68.

5. **Donald Raymond Sandve**, US Army, Staff Sargent, Company C, 1st Battalion, 28th Infantry, 1st Infantry Division. Born November 11, 1932, died January 9, 1966. Died in the same lesser-known place as Pasch—Binh Duong Province, South Vietnam. Sandve was an infantry man who died from an explosive device and was a non-commissioned officer, probably a squad leader. He died within four months of being assigned to the Vietnam conflict. Sandve was born in Britton and raised in Langford. According to information from the *Aberdeen American News*, Sandve entered the service in 1951 and served in the Korean War on two separate occasions and was a 15-year Army veteran. Prior to

Donald Raymond Sandve

being assigned to Vietnam, Sandve was stationed in Germany for three years. He left behind a widow and seven children, a mother, and several brothers and sisters. Sandve is buried in the Groton Cemetery. Donald Raymond Sandve is commemorated on the Wall at Panel 4E, Line 60. The *Groton Independent* indicated that one of Sandve's sisters was a resident of Groton. Another paper indicated that she was a resident of Columbia.

6. **Curtis Leland Williams**, US Army, Specialist 4, 178th ASHC (Assault Support Helicopter Company), 14th Aviation Battalion, 16th Aviation Group, Army. Born September 13, 1951, died February 6, 1971. Died in Quang Tin Province, South Vietnam. Williams died during the crash of his helicopter.

Curtis Leland Williams

Williams was born and raised in Webster and was assigned to Korea for six months prior to being deployed to Vietnam in October 1970. He had been in country approximately five months when he died. He was survived by his parents, two brothers (one of whom was also stationed in Vietnam at the same time), and a sister. Williams was buried in the Webster Cemetery. Curtis Leland Williams is commemorated on the Wall at Panel W5, Line 82. On a side note, because he was not wounded or killed in action, he was not awarded the Purple Heart.

7. **Charles Maury Hallstrom**, US Army, 1st Lieutenant, B Co., 26th Engineer

Charles Hallstrom

Battalion, Americal Division, USARV. Born July 14, 1946 and died September 25, 1970. Hallstrom had been in South Vietman less than three months when he was killed by hostile fire (explosive device) in the Quang Ngai Province. Hallstrom graduated from Webster high school and received his commission while participating in ROTC at the South Dakota State School of Mines and Technology. He had been in the US Army for 16 months prior to being killed. Hallstrom was buried in the Webster Cemetery and was survived by his parents, two brothers, and four sisters. Charles Maury Hallstrom is commemorated on the Wall at Panel W7, Line 89.

8. **Robert Gene Fortin,** US Army, Warrant Officer – Helicopter Pilot, B Troop, 3rd Squadron, 17th Cavalry, 1st Aviation Brigade, USARV. Born November 20, 1949 and died September 13, 1971. Fortin died after his utility/observation helicopter was hit by enemy fire while in flight
Robert Fortin

and his crewmates were unable to get him to a medical facility after the helicopter crashed. He was assigned to South Vietnam in April 1971 and died in September, 1971 in Tay Ninh Province, South Vietnam. He called Turton his home and a brother, Master Sergeant Roger A. Fortin, US Air Force lives in Doland, South Dakota. The weekend before Fortin died, he was joined by his brother for the weekend in Phu Loi, who was also serving in South Vietnam at the time. Robert Gene Fortin is commemorated on the Wall at Panel W2, Line 15.

In addition to those lost in the Vietnam conflict, the following local individuals served in South Vietnam. This is based upon public information. Most Vietnam veterans choose to remain quiet about their military activities or accomplishments. Most if not all of them, (including those who we should consider Vietnam Era Veterans (1962 through 1975) remember most, the lack of attention when they returned home. The looks received in airports when they wore the uniform home. The quiet conversations when they were watched. The terms such as baby killers, etc. Tough times for most. The Vietnam conflict tore this country apart, and they received most of the scorn. Short haircuts, pressed uniforms, and medals on their chest received little or no "thanks for your service." They just came home and quietly faded into the surroundings. We can thank the following individuals for serving in South Vietnam and coming home alive:

SOUTH VIETNAM

1. **Robert M. Barrie**, US Air Force, served in 1968–1972. Barrie was a food service specialist at Cam Ranh Bay Air Force Base, South Vietnam, from February 1969 until February 1970. Basic training at Lackland Air Force Base, Texas; Dover Air Force Base July 1968 until February 1969; and George Air Force Base, California, February 1970 until June 1972 when Barrie was discharged. Awarded Vietnam Service Medal, Vietnam Campaign Medal, and US Air Force Commendation Medal. Graduated from Groton High School in 1966 and graduated from South Dakota State University in 1976.

2. **Keith Baggett,** US Air Force, Master Sergeant, served in 1970 through 1990, Vietnam, Thailand, and Azores. Awarded Meritorious Service/3 Oak Leaf Clusters, Air Force Commendation/2 Oak Leaf Clusters, and Humanitarian Service/6 Oak Leaf Clusters.

3. **Douglas Benedict,** US Navy, Chief Petty Officer Second Class, in June 1968, returned from Vietnam for a 30-day leave with his parents, Mr. and Mrs. DeWayne Benedict of Groton. Had served in the US Navy since December 1965. Benedict is a 1965 graduate of Conde High School. He returned to Vietnam after completion of the leave for an additional six months.

4. **Duane Berreth,** US Army, 1st Lieutenant, in December 1966, became the detachment commander at the 67th Evac Hospital, Qui Nohn, South Vietnam. Berreth was joined by his wife, an Army nurse at the same location. Son of Mr. and Mrs. Ernest Berreth of Groton. Berreth is a 1961 graduate of Groton High School.

5. **Brian W. Carey** US Army, Chief Warrant Officer, Helicopter Pilot, was assigned to the 1st Signal Brigade in South Vietnam in May 1970. Carey entered the Army in November 1968. In October 1970, he was awarded the Air Medal near Nha Trang, South Vietnam, for meritorious service while participating in aerial flight in support of ground operations. Graduated from Groton High School in 1964.

6. **LaVerne J. Debilzan,** US Army, enlisted in 1959, assigned to South Vietnam in September 1968 to II Field Force near Long Binh. Debilzan held the Combat

Infantry Badge, Army Commendation Medal, and the Purple Heart. Debilzan is the son of Mrs. Cele Debilzan of Groton.

Robert Dauwen

7. **Robert Dauwen,** US Navy, Engineer First Class, served 1963 through 1983, and served in Panama and Vietnam. Andover native.

8. **Richard Neil Dresbach,** US Air Force, four years. Served at Stead Air Force Base, Reno, Nevada; Clark Air Force Base, Philippines; Nakhon, Thailand; and South Vietnam. Dresbach was born in Groton and graduated from Groton High School in 1959.

9. **Mike Erickson,** US Navy, information not available.

Mike Erickson

10. **Ronald Falk**, US Army, Specialist 5, B Battery, 2nd Battalion, 23rd Field Artillery, 1st Field Forces, South Vietnam. 1969 through 1970. Falk entered the Army in March 1969 and was stationed in Fort Sill, Oklahoma, prior to being assigned to South Vietnam. Graduated from Groton High School in 1967.

Ronald Falk

11. **Steve Fredrickson**, US Navy, E4, served from 1961 through 1966. Served on the USS *Kearsarge* and received the Expeditionary Medal, Vietnam War Medal, and the National Defense Service Medal.

Steve Fredrickson

12. **Robert J. Hoops**, US Navy, Medic, enlisted in 1965, transferred to orthopedic ward of a military hospital in Da Nang, South Vietnam, in July 1967. Served in Japan prior to the assignment in Vietnam. Graduated from Groton High School in 1965. Son of Mr. and Mrs. James Hoops of Groton.

Robert Hoops

13. **Joel R. Hornaman**, US Army, Specialist 5, assigned to 39th Transportation Battalion as a clerk typist in Da Nang, South Vietnam. Entered the Army in August 1969 after graduating from Northern State College. In 1970, Hornaman received the Army Commendation Medal while serving near Gia Le, South Vietnam. Earned the award for meritorious service as a clerk typist with the battalion's Headquarters Detachment. In January 1971, Hornaman was awarded the Bronze Star Medal and promoted to Specialist 5 for distinguishing himself through meritorious service in connection with military operations against hostile forces. Graduated from Groton High School in 1965.

14. **William Jensen,** US Army, Specialist 4, in November 1971, stationed with the Screaming Eagles at Hue, South Vietnam. Jensen is a graduate of Groton High School. Jensen entered the Army in January 1970.

15. **Charles Johnson**, served in Vietnam, graduated from Groton High School in 1963.

16. **Gordon R. Johnson**, US Navy, MM3, enlisted in 1966. Assigned to the aircraft

Gordon Johnson

carrier, USS *Ranger* CVA-61, in 1967. Stationed at Yankee Station, South Vietnam. Graduated from Columbia High School in 1966. Medals received include Meritorious Unit Commendation, Armed Forces Expeditionary, and Vietnam Campaign/Device. Discharged in 1972.

17. **Paul Karst**, US Marine, 5th Marines/452nd Ord Company, Master Sergeant, served from 1963 through 1997. Chu Lai and Da Nang, South Vietnam.

Paul Karst

18. **Marvin D. Kluck,** US Navy, Lieutenant Commander (Ret), in June 1963, was promoted to lieutenant (JG) while serving with the Western Pacific Detachment, Beachmaster Unit at Yokosuka, Japan. Spoke to his son, Roger Kluck, who indicated that his father served in Danang and Chu Lai. Marvin started his career as the lowest enlisted man and retired after 30 years as Lieutenant Commander and was a submariner. Son of Mr. and Mrs. Gus Kluck of Columbia.

19. **Dale Kurth,** US Army, Claremont High School graduate.

20. **David Krueger**, US Air Force, served from 1963 to 1967. Served in Vietnam.

Dale Kurth

21. **Richard Krueger**, served in Vietnam. Graduated from Groton High School in 1964.

22. **Joseph A. Lange**, US Army, Specialist 5, South Vietnam. Graduated from Groton High School in 1960. Received the Joint Service Commendation Medal during ceremonies

near Saigon, South Vietnam, October 10, 1968. Lange was a reconnaissance non-commissioned officer in the Intelligence Section Reconnaissance Branch at Headquarters US Army Military Assistance Command.

23. **Dennis A. Larson,** US Army, served from 1961 to 1970. Served in Korea and Vietnam. Resident of Groton and a 1961 graduate of Britton High School.

24. **Gerald Lehman**, US Army, Helicopter Crew Chief, served from 1965 through 1967. Camp Enari, South Vietnam. Received an Air Medal with two Oak Leaf Clusters & V (Valor), the Vietnam Service Medal, Vietnam Campaign Medal, the National Defense Service Medal, and an Overseas Service Bar. Lehman graduated from Groton High School in 1963.

Gerald Lehman

25. **Chuck Lowary,** US Air Force, Lieutenant Colonel (Ret), entered the Air Force through Reserve Officer Training Corps (ROTC) at South Dakota State University in 1971. Flew as Naval/Weapons Systems Officer in EC-121 Constellation and F-111 aircraft – flying service at McClellan Air Force Base, California (deployed Korat Royal Thai Air Force Base Thailand, Keflavik Naval Air Station, Iceland), Mountain Home, Idaho, Royal Air Force Upper Heyford, United Kingdom (twice). Awarded Air Medal with two Devices, Vietnam Service Medal with one Device, Republic of Vietnam Gallantry Cross with one Device, and Republic of Vietnam Campaign Medal. Served in support of Operation Desert Shield/Storm. Retired as

a Lieutenant Colonel in 1993. Graduated from Groton High School in 1965.

26. **Donald E. Meints,** US Army, Specialist 5, in December 1966, served with Headquarters Company, 18th Engineer Brigade, South Vietnam. In September 1967, Meints was awarded the Army Commendation Medal for meritorious service as engineer supply clerk specialist in the company. Graduated from Columbia High School in 1963 and son of Mr. and Mrs. F.E. Meints of Columbia.

27. **Dennis F. Meister**, US Army, Specialist 5, received the Army Commendation Medal while serving with the 4th Infantry Division near Pleiku, South Vietnam. Meister earned the award for meritorious service as clerk in Headquarters and Service Battery, 5th Battalion of the Division's 16th Artillery. Entered the Army in September 1965 and was stationed in Italy before being assigned to South Vietnam. Graduated from Groton High School.

28. **Gerald Meister,** US Navy, Boatswain's Mate Second Class, in February 1968, received a citation for outstanding performance of duty while attached to and serving on the USS *Okinawa* from April to November 1967 during combat operations against the enemy. Son of Mr. and Mrs. Ervin Meister of Groton. He had been in the Navy for approximately seven years.

29. **Ron Mielke**, US Army, Captain, Combat Engineering, South Vietnam, from October 1965 until September 1966. Graduated from South Dakota State University and received an ROTC commission as 2nd Lieutenant

from South Dakota State's Army Reserve Officers' Training Corps. Left active duty in September 1967 and joined South Dakota National Guard as a captain in 1972. Retired in 2002 as a brigadier general. Graduated from Groton High School in 1960. Son of Harvey and Louise Mielke of Groton.

30. **Dennis D. Mitchell,** US Army, promoted to Sergeant 1969. Mitchell was a clerk in Company D., 3rd Battalion of the 25th Infantry Division near Tay Ninh, South Vietnam. Arrived in South Vietnam in March 1968 and held the Army Commendation Medal for heroism. Graduated from Columbia High School in 1963 and received a BA Degree from Northern State College in 1967.

31. **Ronald E. Neitzel,** US Air Force, Staff Sergeant, in November 1972, was a member of an Air Training Command organization at Shepard Air Force Base, Texas. He was an aircraft maintenance instructor with the 3750th Technical School. He is a 1967 graduate of Groton High School and has completed a tour of duty in Vietnam. Son of Mr. and Mrs. Burton Neitzel of Groton.

32. **James Neuhardt**, US Army, Infantry Small Arms Specialist, South Vietnam in 1965.

33. **Gerald L. Paetznick,** US Air Force, Technical Sergeant, was a refrigeration and air conditioning specialist assigned to Cam Ranh Bay Air Force Base, South Vietnam, in 1969. Graduated from Groton High School in 1948. Son of Mr. and Mrs. Oscar Paetznick of Groton.

34. **Berwyn Place**, US Army, Colonel (Ret), a career solder. Received the Legion of Merit, Bronze Star, Vietnam Service Medal, Army Service Ribbon, Overseas Service Ribbon, and Republic of Vietnam Campaign Medal, among others.

35. **Donald Protas**, US Army, South Vietnam in 1962, and in Germany. Received the Bronze Star and Army Commendation Medal (s). Died in 2019 after a four-year battle with lung cancer, due to exposure to Agent Orange, while he was stationed in Vietnam.

36. **Jerry Raap**, US Army, Specialist 4, 58th Transportation, Fort Leonard Wood, Missouri, and South Vietnam. Received draft notice in November 1963. Reported to Fort Leonard Wood, Missouri, for basic training. Boarded a troop train in Missouri to travel to California for the ultimate departure for South Vietnam.

    Jerry Raap

    Train stopped in Montana so local cowboys could sell beer to the thirsty soldiers. Arrived in California where protestors stopped the train. Trip to Vietnam took 22 days with salt-water showers. Storage containers with gear got lost, and the first issue of ammunition was three rounds each, and there were no tents to sleep in. Raap indicated to fix that problem; they did it the Army way. They stole tents. His unit was a transportation unit and hauled supplies from Qui Nhon to Pleiku and AnKhe and were escorted by helicopters and infantry soldiers. His enlistment ended four months later. No celebration or fanfare when he arrived back in country. Served from 1963 through 1965. Graduated from Andover High School in 1959.

37. **John A. Raap**, US Army, Specialist 4, promoted in 1967 while serving near Da Nang, South Vietnam. Raap was a clerk for Company A, 37th Signal Battalion. Raap entered the Army in June 1966 and also served in Fort Gordon, Georgia. Graduated from Groton High School in 1963.

38. **Larry Ragels**, US Army, assigned to South Vietnam in August 1968. Severely wounded and received the Purple Heart from actions in September 1968. Recovery took months. He was discharged in March 1974. Ragels graduated from Groton High School in 1965.

39. **William "Bill" Reinhardt,** US Army, enlisted along with Clyde Hansen from Groton/Columbia. Bill went to basic training in Fort Leonard Wood, Missouri, and his advanced training was in Fort Ord, California, where he was trained as an infantry radio operator. Bill did a tour in South Vietnam. Graduated from Warner High School in 1970. Son of Duane and Donna Reinhardt of Stratford.

40. **Freddie Robinson,** US Army, Chief Warrant Officer 4, in May 1966, served a year in South Vietnam with the 79th Artillery at On Son Nhut Airbase at Saigon. Served in Germany the previous 22 months. Completed basic training in Fort Leonard Wood, Missouri. Son of Mr.

Freddie Robinson

and Mrs. Allen Robinson of Stratford. Graduate of Warner High School. Served 1963 through 2002.

41. **Robert E. Rystrom**, US Army, Lieutenant Colonel (Ret), served 1969-1990. Promoted to captain in 1971 while serving as senior military advisor to the MACV Advisory Team, Hieu Duc, South Vietnam. Awarded Bronze Star, Vietnam Service, and Meritorious Service medals. Graduated from Columbia High School and was a 1969 graduate of the University of South Dakota.

Robert Rystrom

42. **Robert A. Sanders,** US Marine, Lance Corporal, in December 1966, served with H Company, Second Battalion, First Marine Division, Da Nang, South Vietnam. Son of Mr. and Mrs. Arnold J. Sanders of Stratford.

43. **Jerral W. Serr,** US Army, Private First Class, in September 1965, assigned to the US Army, South Vietnam, as a clerk. Entered the Army in May 1964 and received basic training at Fort Leonard Wood, Missouri. 1960 graduate of Aberdeen Central. Son of Mr. and Mrs. Walter Serr of Columbia.

44. **James M. Serr,** US Navy, Machinist's Mate Third Class, was a crew member of the USS *Perkins*, 7th Fleet, which successfully engaged in a running battle with North Vietnamese shore batteries. Son of Mr. and Mrs. Walter Serr of Columbia.

45. **Kenneth Sieber,** US Army, Specialist 4, returned home from Vietnam in June 1966. Served at An Khe in the

central highlands of South Vietnam. Entered the Army in 1964 and took basic training in Fort Leonard Wood, Missouri. Graduate of Columbia High School and son of Mr. and Mrs. Walter Sieber of Columbia.

46. **Dennis Sombke**, US Air Force, Captain, was assigned to Phu Cat Air Force Base in South Vietnam in December 1970. Graduated from Groton High School in 1957. Son of Mr. and Mrs. Edward Sombke of Ferney.

47. **Ron Spencer**, US Air Force, from 1969 through 1972. Stationed at Chanute Air Force Base and Lockland Air Base, California. In December 1970, he was assigned to the 35th Civil Engineering Squadron in Phan Rang, South Vietnam. Graduated from Claremont High School in 1967.

48. **Gerald K. Sundling**, served in South Vietnam and graduated from Groton High School in 1966.

49. **Dennis Swanson,** US Marines, Sergeant, served from June 1964 through May 1968, Danang Air Base, non-crew aviation Ordnance flying C130 flare ship. Air medial with five stars. 1961 graduate of Groton High School. Son of Oscar and Irene Swanson.

50. **Scott Thomas,** veteran of service in South Vietnam.

51. **Larry Wegner**, US Air Force, Captain, Young Tigers 4252D Strategic Wing, Strategic Air Command (SAC), and flew in Vietnam for a year during his service term. In November 1964, entered US Air Force pilot training at Webb

Larry Wegner

Air Force Base, Texas. Wegner received his commission upon completion of the Reserve Officer Training Corps program at South Dakota State College where he graduated with a B.S. degree in economics. Served from 1966 through 1969. Graduated from Groton High School in 1959. Son of Mr. and Mrs. Robert S. Wegner of Groton.

52. **Neil Wagner,** US Navy, Engineman 3rd Class, served from November 1967 through December 1970. Enlisted in Navy shortly after receiving his draft notice. Assigned to USS *Mercer* APB 39 and stationed in the waters around Cambodia and South Vietnam. USS *Mercer* was a barracks/hospital ship. Received Combat Action Ribbon.

53. **Alan E. Wockenfuss,** US Air Force, Lieutenant Colonel, in September 1966, was commander of the 308th Tactical Fighter Squadron, known as the Emerald Knights. Led a sortie that destroyed three buildings and damaged 15 others. It marked the 5,000th sortie in South Vietnam for the squadron.

VIETNAM ERA from February 1962 to May 1975

Based upon my review of news for this period and conversations with veterans, the following individuals served during the Vietnam Era but not in South Vietnam.

1. **James O. Barrie,** US Air Force, Technical Sergeant, in June 1965, promoted while stationed at Larson Air Force Base, Washington. Son of Mr. and Mrs. Leon J. Barrie of Turton.

2. **Emmet P. Bakke,** US Air Force, Staff Sergeant, in May 1973, graduated at Lowry Air Force Base, CO, from the Air Force precision measuring equipment specialist course conducted by the Air Training Command. His wife, Karen, is the daughter of Mr. and Mrs. Wayne Sanderson of Groton.

3. **Gary Baule**, US Army.

4. **Clarence F. Beauvals,** in July 1964, Army Reserve Officer Training Corps cadet underwent six weeks of military training at Fort Lewis, Washington. Son of Mr. and Mrs. Fred J. Beauvals of Turton.

5. **Curtis Belden,** Lieutenant JG, National Oceanic and Atmospheric Administration (NOAA) from April 1972 through May 1975. Graduated from South Dakota School of Mines in 1971 with a degree in Geological Engineering and was commissioned as an ensign in NOAA in April 1972. Took officer training at the US Merchant Marine Academy at Kings Point, Long Island, New York. Conducted oceanographic research on Lake Ontario and the North-Atlantic Ocean from the Florida Keys to Dakar, Senegal in West Africa. As chief geophysical officer, research included some of the first deep ocean photography of the Mid-Atlantic Ridge undersea volcanic activity. In 1974, he was assigned to the NOAA National Geodetic Survey and managed land-based survey crews along the East Coast. Graduated from Groton High School in 1967.

6. **David Belden**, US Navy, served in the mid-1960s. Graduated from Andover High School.

7. **Thomas H. Belden,** US Air Force, Airman, in November 1964, completed the first phase of his Air Force basic military training at Lackland Air Force Base, Texas. Selected for technical training as an aircraft equipment repairman at the Air Training Command School at Chanute Air Force Base, Illinois. Belden is a 1961 graduate of Groton High School and son of Mr. and Mrs. Harold H. Belden of Groton.

    Thomas H. Belden

8. **Lanny Beyer**, US Air Force, served from 1963 to 1967. Stationed at Minot airbase. Graduated from Groton High School in 1962.

9. **David G. Blackmun,** US Army, Private, in November 1964, completed a field communication crewman course under the Reserve Enlistment Program at Fort Leonard Wood, Missouri. Son of Mr. and Mrs. Earl O. Blackmun and graduated from Groton High School in 1961.

10. **Tom Blair,** US Army, retired as captain.

11. **Robert Boehmer**, US Army, Specialist 4, HHC VII Corps, Germany. Served from 1972 through 1974. National Defense Service Medal. Graduated from Groton High School in 1968.

    Tom Blair

12. **Charles H. Bohling,** US Army, Private, in November 1974 enlisted in the Army's Delayed Entry Program

and reported in May 1975. A 1970 graduate of Groton High School and completed two years of study at South Dakota State University prior to enlistment. Son of Mr. and Mrs. Harvey H. Bohling of Columbia.

13. **Michael W. (Mick) Brown,** US Army, Staff Sergeant, served in Germany and various units in US. Discharged in 1977 after seven years of service. A 1969 Groton High School graduate.

14. **Dale Buntrock,** US Army Reserve, Specialist 5, served from 1971 through 1977. A 1969 graduate of Groton High School.

15. **Larry (Bomber) Buntrock,** US Navy, served from 1964 through 1968. Basic training at Great Lakes Naval Training Station. Assigned to USS *Sperry*, a submarine supply ship then assigned to USS *ARD-BS-20*, a dry dock ship for an underwater research submarine. He is a 1961 graduate of Groton High School. Served during the Vietnam conflict but feels fortunate that he did not have to go to South Vietnam. Son of LaVern (Rocky) and Maxine Buntrock of Groton.

16. **Kenneth L. Campbell,** US Air Force, Staff Sergeant, in July 1968, graduated from US Air Force technical school at Keesler Air Force Base, Mississippi. He was trained as a radio repairman and was assigned to a unit of the Pacific Air Forces at Clark Air Force Base, Philippines. Son of Mr. and Mrs. Wallace Campbell and a graduate of Groton High School.

17. **Lester J. Dauwen,** US Army, Private, in December 1966, completed a field communication crewman course at Fort Ord, California. Son of Mr. and Mrs. Joseph C. Dauwen of Andover.

18. **Denny Davies,** US Navy, served from 1973 through 1977. Enlisted in Army National Guard in 1979 and served for the next 18 years. In 1980, Davies moved to Groton and was employed at Darrel's Sinclair and later began a 23-year career with the Groton Area School District as custodian.

19. **Allan B. Dayton,** US Army, Private, in February 1971, completed eight weeks of basic training at the US Army Training Center Infantry, Fort Lewis, Washington. Dayton is a 1968 graduate of Groton High School and son of Mr. and Mrs. Ben F. Dayton of Columbia.

20. **Stephen Dresbach**, Lieutenant Colonel (Ret), US Army Medical Service Corp 1969-1972. Served as a social work officer in the Mental Health Clinic, Martin Army Hospital, Fort Benning, Georgia. Army reserve officer from 1988 to 2004, served in an Army clearing hospital and in combat stress control units around the Midwest. Retired at the rank of lieutenant colonel. Graduated from Groton High School in 1962.

Stephen Dresbach

21. **Douglas G. Ehrenberg,** US Army, Private, in March 1965 assigned to Headquarters Battery of the 18th Artillery 4th Howitzer Battalion in

Douglas G. Ehrenberg

Germany as a wireman. Entered the Army in September 1964 and completed basic training at Fort Leonard Wood, Missouri. 1960 graduate of Andover High School and son of Mr. and Mrs. George H. Ehrenberg of Andover.

22. **Clayton Farmen,** US National Guard, active for 10 years. Employed by Ken's Super Fair Foods at the time of his death in 2003.

Clayton Farmen

23. **Calvin Farmer,** US Air Force, served from 1968 through 1972. He served overseas in England, as a maintenance analysis specialist.

24. **Errol Farmer,** no information available.

25. **James Feist,** US Army, served in Germany. Feist was employed by the City of Groton.

26. **Leslie A. Feller,** US Army, Private, in March 1968, completed a wheeled vehicle mechanic course at Fort Ord, California. Son of Mr. and Mrs. Wayne L. Feller of Groton.

27. **Darrel Fliehs,** US Army, 1966. Graduated from Groton High School in 1964.

Darrel Fliehs

28. **Wally Fisher,** US Army, served in 1963 and discharged in 1965. Spent time on active duty in Germany. Active reserve 1965-1969.

29. **Dennis Furman,** South Dakota Army National Guard, First Sergeant, 1972-2004,

Wally Fisher

Korea, Gulf War, and Iraq. Awarded Army Commendation (3), Kuwait Liberation (2), and Operation Iraqi Freedom. Native of Groton.

30. **Darwin Furst**, US Air Force, 1965.

31. **Joe Gentry**, US Navy. Graduated from Groton High School in 1967.

32. **Robert L. Gildy,** US Air Force, Cadet, in August 1962, participated in Air Force Reserve Officer Training Corps summer encampment. Son of Mr. and Mrs. Leonard A. Gildy of Groton. Gildy was a member of the South Dakota State College Air Force Reserve Officer Training Corps program and eligible for appointment as an Air Force second lieutenant upon graduation.

33. **Kaye P. Gooding,** US Army Women's Army Corp, Private, in February 1967, completed eight weeks of basic training at Fort McClellan, Alabama. Daughter of Clifford Gannon of Andover.

34. **Jerry D. Gooding,** US Army, Sergeant, served in 1965 until 1971, Co C. 3rd Battalion 51st Infantry, Advanced Marksmanship Unit, US Army Europe, Fort Knox, Kentucky, and Erlangen Germany. Son of Mr. and Mrs. William H. Gooding of Andover. A 1961 graduate of Andover High School.

35. **Morris O. Gosa,** US Air Force, Staff Sergeant, in June 1964, arrived for duty with a unit of the US Air Force in Europe at Bitburg Air Force Base, Germany, as a transportation supervisor. Married to Marion Lindert, daughter of Mr. and Mrs. George Lindert of Groton.

36. **Clyde Hansen,** US Army, enlisted in December 1970. Basic training at Fort Leonard Wood, Missouri, and took advanced training as an Artillery Survey Specialist in Fort Sill, Oklahoma. Then completed airborne training with the 82nd Airborne at Fort Benning, Georgia. Permanent duty station was in Fort Benning. Graduated from Groton High School in 1970 and son of Delmar and Gladys Hansen, who lived on a farm near Columbia.

Clyde Hansen

37. **Michael M. Hansen,** US Army, Specialist 4, served in 1966 to 1968 in Germany. Native of Stratford.

38. **Lawrence E. Harry**, US Army, completed basic training at Fort Campbell, Kentucky, in June 1971. Graduated from Groton High School in 1969.

39. **Ronald Harry,** US Army, Fort Gordon, Georgia. Native of Ferney and graduate of Groton High School.

40. **Bob Hein**, US Army, Specialist 4, Medic, served in Germany from 1966 through 1968. December 1966 completed eight weeks of basic medical training at Fort Huachuca, Arizona. Hein was trained in first aid, caring for patients in wards, preventive medicine, and medical skills necessary in assisting doctors and nurses in medical work. Son of Mr. and Mrs. Wilbert R. Hein of Groton. A 1965 Andover High School graduate. The last graduation class of Andover High School before it was consolidated with Groton.

Bob Hein

41. **Gary Hellman,** no information available.

42. **Rod Hinrichs,** US Army, served in Germany from 1971 through 1974. National Defense Service Medal and Army Commendation Medal. Graduated from Claremont High School in 1967 and resident of Groton.

43. **Gilbert Hinkelman,** US Army, Private, in September 1963, completed an eight-week power man course at the Engineer Center, Fort Belvoir, Virginia. Entered the Army in April 1963 and received basic training at Fort Leonard Wood, Missouri. A 1958 graduate of Groton High School and son of Mr. and Mrs. Herbert Hinkelman of Groton.

Gilbert Hinkelman

44. **Ronald W. Hoffman,** US Army, served three years in Fort Monmouth, New Jersey, and in Lenggries, Germany.

45. **Dennis N. Hornaman,** US Air Force, Airman Second Class, following graduation from technical training course for US Air Force radio equipment repairmen in April 1964, was assigned to Las Vegas Air Force Station, Nevada. Son of Mr. and Mrs. Herbert Hornaman of Groton, and a graduate of Groton High School.

46. **Charles Hoops**, US Army, Specialist 4, in May 1975, assigned as a heavy truck driver in the 180th Transportation Battalion, Fort Hood, Texas. Served 1972–1975. 1972 Groton High School graduate. Son of Mr. and Mrs. Charles H. Hoops of Groton.

47. **Gary Hoops**, US Navy, served from 1971 through 1975. Served abroad the USN *John F. Kennedy*. Enlisted in Navy after receiving his draft notice. A 1969 Groton High School graduate.

Gary Hoops

48. **David Hosley**, US Army, Major (Ret) enlisted in April 1972 and in January 1994, was discharged and retired as a major. Most interesting assignment was an executive officer in a maintenance battalion in Queens, New York. Graduated from Groton High School in 1971.

49. **Terrance C. Hubbard**, US Navy. 1960 graduate of the US Naval Academy.

50. **Kenneth V. Janisch**, US Air Force, Sergeant, assigned to Ellsworth Air Force Base in July 1970 as a supply supervisor with the 821st Combat Support Group. Graduated from Andover High School and married to Jeanette Pray, daughter of Robert C. Pray Sr. of Groton.

51. **Peter Jahraus,** US Marine, Rifle Sharpshooter and Merit Mast, completed Aerographers Mate Class A in 1973. Weather Observer with secondary Aircraft Mechanic. Graduate of Pierre Riggs High School in 1972 and South Dakota State University in 1980. Married to Susan Raines Jahraus, daughter of Donley and Marion Raines, Groton, SD. Attended boot camp in San Diego, CA and stationed in Camp Pendleton, CA, Iwakuni, Japan, and New River, NC.

Peter Jahraus

52. **Eugene Johnson,** US Marines, E-4, served in Okinawa from 1975 through 1978. Raised in Columbia.

53. **Glenn H. Johnson,** US Army, Private, in September 1963 completed a seven-week petroleum storage specialist course at the Quartermaster Center, Fort Lee, Virginia. Johnson entered the Army in April 1963 and received basic training at Fort Leonard Wood, Missouri. Served as a fuel specialist in France and Germany. Discharged in 1965. Son of Mr. and Mrs. Chester Johnson of Groton.

54. **Kenneth R. Johnson,** US Air Force, Staff Sergeant, in July 1966, promoted as a radio repairman at Waverly Air Base Station, Iowa. Graduate of Groton High School and son of Mr. and Mrs. Ronald Hubbard of Groton.

55. **Lyle Johnson**, US Army.

56. **Richard L. Johnson,** US Army, Private, in August 1965, completed eight weeks of military police training at the Army Training Center, Fort Gordon, Georgia. Entered the Army in March 1965 and was discharged in 1971. A 1961 graduate of Groton High School. Son of Mr. and Mrs. Chester C. Johnson of Groton.

57. **Dana L. Jones,** US Army, Private, in February 1971, graduated from five-week light vehicle driver course at Fort Ord, California. Jones entered the Army in July 1970. A 1968 graduate of Groton High School and received a diploma from the Lake Area Technical School in 1970. He is the son of Mr. and Mrs. Gwynne Jones of Bath.

58. **Owen Jones**, US Army, Lieutenant Colonel (Ret) attended South Dakota State University on a ROTC scholarship and commissioned as a 2nd Lieutenant and after officer basic was assigned to the 8th Infantry Division in Germany. Assigned to the Ordnance Branch. Twenty-two years of service including stops in Germany, Aberdeen Proving Grounds, Maryland, and as Professor of Military Science ROTC Kent State University, among others. Retired from the military as a Lieutenant Colonel. A 1971 graduate of Groton High School.

Owen Jones

59. **Cloyd Kanaly,** US Marines, Sergeant, served from 1966 through 1969, native of Columbia.

60. **Larry R. Karlen,** US Marines, 1st Lieutenant, in July 1960, underwent pre-flight training at the Naval Air Station, Pensacola, Florida. Ten-week training in aviation science, navigation, principles of flight and other technical courses to prepare for their future as naval aviators. In October 1963, Karlen participated in joint training with Pacific Fleet Amphibious Forces. Son of Mr. and Mrs. Rudy Karlen of Columbia.

61. **Bob Karlen,** US Army, Captain, entered the Army in 1971 after being commissioned as a 2nd Lieutenant via the ROTC program at the University of South Dakota. Served on active duty until 1976, at which time joined the National Guard at Fort Richardson, Alaska. Retired after 24 years of service as a colonel. Son of Mr. and Mrs. Edwin Karlen of Columbia.

62. **Amy Kaufman**, US Air Force, Airman, in September 1969 graduated from the US Air Force technical school at Sheppard Air Force Base, Texas. Trained as a medical services specialist. Graduate of Groton High School and attended Lake Area Vocational Technical School in Watertown.

63. **Charles J. Kellison,** US Army, Private, in March 1966 completed eight-weeks of military police training. Kellison, 1963 graduate of Groton High School, entered the Army in October 1965. Son of Mrs. A. Kellison of Groton.

64. **Ronald Kluck,** US Air Force, served four years and discharged in 1965. Ronald was an airplane mechanic who worked for TWA after his discharge. Son of Mr. and Mrs. Gus Kluck. A 1961 graduate of Columbia High School.

65. **Elmer J. Knecht,** US Army, Private, in December 1964, completed a 14-week automotive repair course at the Army Armor Center, Fort Knox, Kentucky. Knecht entered the Army in June 1964 and completed basic training at Fort Leonard Wood, Missouri. A 1960 graduate of Claremont High School and resident of Houghton.

66. **Dwight Allan Knoll,** US Army, enlisted after graduating from Warner High School in 1967. Served in Korea. Grew up in Groton and attended country school and high school in Warner.

67. **Glenn Kraai,** served in Germany. Formerly of Andover.

68. **Laurence Krieger,** US Army, served from 1961 to 1963. Graduated from Andover High School in 1956.

69. **Howie A. Krienke**, US Army, 2nd Lieutenant, in 1970 completed a nine-week chaplain officer basic course at the US Army Chaplain School, Fort Hamilton, New York. His wife, Linda, lived in Groton at that time.

70. **David Krueger,** US Army, Captain, enlisted in March 1973 and served through March of 1975. Served in US Army reserves until December 1978, during which he was promoted to captain. Attended grade schools in Ferney and graduated from Groton High School in 1968.

71. **Hugo Kryger,** US Navy, served in 1966 to 1970. Graduated from Groton High School in 1962.

72. **Paul R. Keup,** US Army, Private, in June 1967 completed a field communications crewman course at Fort Ord, California. Son of Mr. and Mrs. Reinhard Keup of Andover.

73. **Hank Kurtz,** US Air Force, joined after graduating from Groton High School in 1965. Served as a flight crewman for medical evacuations during the Vietnam War.

74. **Gerald Lakemaker**, US Army, commissioned as a 2nd Lieutenant in 1967 after graduating from Officer Candidate School (OCS). In June 1960, he was in class of cadets receiving six weeks training of the Army Reserve Officer Training Corps summer camp at Fort Riley, Kansas. Lakemaker served until 1966. A 1957

graduate of Groton High School. Son of Mr. and Mrs. Martin E. Lakemaker of Groton.

75. **Dennis D. Larson**, US Marine, Private, in February 1962 completed recruit training at the Marine Corps Recruit Depot, San Diego, California. Larson was assigned to Camp Pendleton, California, for infantry training. Son of Mr. and Mrs. Andrew Larson of Andover. Discharged in 1966. Graduated from Groton High School in 1961.

76. **Jerry Larson,** US Army, 1961 graduate of Columbia High School.

77. **Ray Larson,** US Army Reserves, 1972–1978. Basic training and AIT in Fort Polk, Louisiana, from November 1972 until March 1973. His selective service number was 99 and Selective Service drafted up to 100. Ray was one of the last draftees from Brown County during the Vietnam conflict. Ray and his wife Cyndy were married one month before he got his letter from the Selective Service.

Ray Larson

78. **Keith D. Lawson,** US Army, Private, in May 1974 completed eight-weeks of basic training at the US Army Training Center, Infantry, Fort Polk, Louisiana. Son of Perry Lawson of Groton.

79. **Sheldon Lenling**, US Air Force, Staff Sergeant, in August 1969, was promoted to staff sergeant and assigned to Beate Air Force Base, California, a unit of the

Sheldon Lenling

strategic air command. A 1962 graduate of Groton High School.

80. **Larry Liedholt,** US Army, served from August 1966 to August 1968. Resident of Groton at his death.

81. **David McGannon**, 1970 Groton High School graduate.

82. **Robert McGannon,** US Army National Guard for four years.

83. **Jacky Dale McKiver**, US Army, Private, in November 1972, completed eight-weeks of basic training at the US Army Training Center, Armor, Fort Knox, Kentucky. After a long career with the National Guard, McKiver retired under a medical retirement. 1970 Groton High School graduate. Son of Mr. and Mrs. Dale McKiver of Groton.

Jacky Dale McKiver

84. **Dale E. Meister,** US Air Force, Airman Third Class, in June 1964 was shot and killed at Ellsworth Air Force Base, South Dakota. Died while on guard duty with two gunshot wounds to his chest. The bullets came from his own weapon. He had been in the Air Force for approximately 18 months. Services for Meister were conducted at St. John's Lutheran Church in Groton. He was buried in Union Cemetery.

85. **Merle E. Messing**, US Army, Staff Sergeant, South Dakota National Guard, in September 1964, served with the Army at Fort Sill, Oklahoma. During his tour

of duty, he received three letters of commendations. He was selected as the outstanding trainee of his unit.

86. **Bradley Micko,** US Army, served from 1970 until 1978. Graduated from Claremont High School in 1969.

87. **Lambert Mielke,** US Army. 1960 graduate of Groton High School. Son of Roy and Louise Mielke.

88. **Jerry Millim,** US Army, enlisted in 1968 and was discharged in 1971. Served in Korea as a mechanic and other duties. Resident of Groton.

89. **Thomas A. Moody,** US Marines, Corporal, completed 10-months of studying the Vietnamese language at the Defense Language Institute in Washington, DC. Son of Mrs. Eleanor Moody of Columbia. Moody is a graduate of Columbia High School and entered the military in January 1965.

90. **Larry Neubauer,** US Air Force, 1961 graduate of Columbia High School.

91. **Jack Oliver**, South Dakota National Guard.

Jack Oliver

92. **James Olson,** US Air Force, in September 1966, enlisted in the US Air Force in the administrative and mechanical area.

93. **Lynette M. Olsen,** US Navy, Ensign, in November 1964, completed the indoctrination class for women Naval officers at the Naval School Command Naval Base, Newport, Rhode Island. Daughter of Mr. and Mrs. E. Merrile Olson of Columbia. Olsen is also a

graduate of Northern State College in Aberdeen, South Dakota.

94. **Gerald Osterman,** US Army Reserve, October 1962 until October 1968. Attended basic training at Fort Leonard Wood, Missouri. 1959 graduate of Groton High School.

Gerald Osterman

95. **Mel Ott**, 1960 Groton High School graduate.

96. **Lane G. Peterson,** US Army, Private, in October 1964, completed a nine-week basic military journalist course at the Defense Information School, Fort Slocum, New York. Peterson entered the military in April 1964 and completed basic training at Fort Leonard Wood, Missouri. Graduated from Groton High School in 1961. Son of Mr. and Mrs. Leonard M. Peterson of Groton.

97. **Bert Pigors**, US Navy, served in 1971 through 1975.

98. **Brad Pigors**, US Air Force, served in Thailand. After discharge, Pigors entered US Army, serving over 20 years until retirement. A 1968 graduate of Groton High School.

99. **Greg L. Pigors,** US Air Force, Airman, in March 1971 completed basic training at Lackland Air Force Base, Texas. Assigned to Keesler Air Force Base, Mississippi, for training in the communications field. In October 1971, Pigors completed a 23-week course and was assigned to the security squadron at Shemya Air Force Base, Aleutian Islands, Alaska. Pigors is a 1970 graduate of Groton High School and son of Ewald W. Pigors of Groton.

100. **Howard Pigors**, no information available.

101. **Warren Pigors,** US Army, Staff Sergeant, in 1981 was stationed in Fort Carson, Colorado.

102. **Larry Pigors**, US Air Force, served from 1965 through 1969. Served in Guam. 1964 Groton High School graduate.

103. **Patrick T. Prunty,** US Navy, Midshipmen, son of Mr. and Mrs. Ed Prunty of Andover. In October 1970, Prunty was among 50 new freshmen sworn into the Naval Reserve Officer Training Corps program.

104. **Wayne Quiggle Jr.,** South Dakota National Guard, 1961 Groton High School graduate. Quiggle is shown in a picture dated in June 1968 "Legion Honors Vietnam Veterans." The description indicates that Quiggle was a veteran of Vietnam. Unable to confirm. Enlisted in National Guard after graduating from high school and served many years.

105. **Larry D. Rabine,** US Marines, served from 1960 until 1964. Graduated from Andover High School in 1958.

106. **Lee T. Raines**, Specialist 5, US Army, served from 1972 through 1976. HHC V Corps, G1, Frankfurt, Germany. Army Commendation Medal, Good Conduct Medal, and National Defense Service Medal. 1971 Groton High School graduate.

Lee Raines

107. **Lyle Reder,** South Dakota National Guard, discharged in 1970. Attended school in Groton and was employed at Eddy's High-Grade Station, Groton Farm Store, and was parts manager at Trail Chevrolet until his health forced him to retire.

108. **Rick L. Reber,** US Army, Private, in April 1972, completed eight-week basic training at the US Army Training Center, Infantry, Fort Polk, Louisiana. Reber is a 1970 graduate of Groton High School and son of Mr. and Mrs. Walter Reber of Groton.

109. **David Reinhardt**, US Army, Specialist 5, Fort Knox, Kentucky. Received draft notice in December 1970. In the draft drawing of 1969, he received number 16. Had orders for South Vietnam, but orders were superseded by an assignment to Fort Knox. Two years active duty plus four years in the inactive reserves. Graduated from Groton High School in 1969.

110. **Allen F. Ringgenberg,** US Navy, Petty Officer Second Class, served from 1960 through 1963, in August 1963, served aboard USS *Arcadia* on four months deployment with the 6th Fleet in the Mediterranean. Son of Mr. and Mrs. Arthur Ringgenberg of Columbia.

Allen Ringgenberg

111. **Russell A. Rock,** US Army, Private, in January 1963, participated with the 25th Infantry Division in a three-week training exercise in Hawaii. Rock was a truck driver in Hawaii. Son of Mrs. Laverle M. Siefkes of Groton.

112. **Jim Rose**, US Air Force, served in 1963 through 1967. Graduated from Groton High School in 1962.

113. **Myron H. Rose,** US Air Force, served from 1961 to 1967. Graduated from Groton High School in 1961.

Jim Rose

114. **Duane Rude,** US Air Force, served from 1971 to 1974. Lived in Groton prior to his death in 2015.

115. **John Saunders**, US Navy, 1970 Groton High School graduate.

116. **James W. Savage,** US Air Force, Master Sergeant, in November 1964, was presented the Strategic Air Command Aerospace Education Medallion at Homestead Air Force Base, Florida. His wife, Darlene, is the daughter of Mr. and Mrs. John W. Allen of Groton.

117. **Arthur E. Schlenker,** US Army, Private, in June 1965 completed a pay specialist course at the Army Adjutant General School, Fort Benjamin Harrison, Indiana. Entered the Army in November 1964 and completed basic training at Fort Leonard Wood, Missouri. A 1964 graduate of Groton High School.

118. **Bruce T. Schoonover**, US Army, promoted in 1970 to private first class while undergoing individual combat training in Fort Ord, California. Graduated from Barnard High School and the son of Mr. and Mrs. Lyle Schoonover. Was married to Patricia Wolforth all of Columbia. Stayed active in the military via the

National Guard, and Schoonover was activated from the National Guard and was in Iraq during Desert Storm. He passed away in 2020.

119. **Gary L. Sieber,** US Army, Private. In March 1962, Sieber received eight weeks of advanced individual training with the 100th Division at Fort Chaffee, Alaska. A 1956 graduate of Columbia High School and son of Mr. and Mrs. Walter W. Sieber of Columbia.

120. **Kenneth L. Sieber,** US Army, Private, in December 1963, completed a 10-week ammunition storage course at the Army Ordinance Center and School, Aberdeen Proving Ground, Maryland. 1960 graduate of Columbia High School and son of Mr. and Mrs. Walter W. Sieber of Columbia.

121. **Robert Sieber,** US Air Force, Airman First Class, in March 1964, was promoted to airman first class. Served in Thailand during the Vietnam War, and it was his responsibility to check the hydraulics on planes after the planes returned from dropping Agent Orange in Vietnam. Robert contracted liver cancer, which was linked to his exposure to Agent Orange. He eventually succumbed to the cancer at the age of 70. Another death (indirect) attributed to the war in South Vietnam. Son of Mr. and Mrs. Vern Sieber of Columbia. A 1961 graduate of Columbia High School.

122. **Gary Sombke,** US Air Force, Sergeant First Class (Technical), 1971 through 1975, served in Thailand. 1971 graduate of Groton High School.

Gary Sombke

123. **Verlin Stange,** US Army, Private First Class, served from 1959 through 1965, native of Stratford.

124. **Edward Stauch**, South Dakota National Guard, 1960 Groton High School graduate.

Ed Stauch

125. **Donald L. Stroh,** US Army, 2nd Lieutenant, in February 1964 assigned to the 1st Armored Division at Fort Hood, Texas. A 1957 graduate of Groton High School, 1962 graduate of South Dakota School of Mines and Technology, and son of Mr. and Mrs. G. Stroh of Groton.

126. **Daryl Sundermeyer,** Sergeant, South Dakota Army Reserve, served six years. A 1965 graduate of Andover High School. Daughter, Marisa (Sundermeyer) Roemmich, 2008 graduate of Groton High School, joined the South Dakota National Guard in 2008, is an E5, and remains in the guard.

127. **Robert W. Sundermeyer,** July 1964 Army Reserve Officer Training Corps cadet, participated in six weeks of military training at Fort Lewis, Washington. Sundermeyer is the son of Mr. and Mrs. Verne Sundermeyer of Groton.

128. **Robert Sundling**, US Army, Germany, served from February 1966 through January 1968. 1964 graduate of Groton High School.

129. **David Von Wald**, US Navy. Communications technician from 1970 through 1974, stationed in Guam monitoring and locating Russian submarines. A 1965 graduate of Groton High School.

David Von Wald

130. **Greg Von Wald**, US Marines, Lieutenant Colonel (Ret). While in college at the University of South Dakota (USD), Von Wald went into the Marine Corps reserves in 1968. Commissioned in 1971 after graduating from USD. Requested and received orders for South Vietnam, but orders were changed when the last of the US Marines pulled out of South Vietnam. Assigned to 3rd Marine Division in Okinawa in 1973 through 1974. Two combat tours. One in Lebanon as a Military Observer with the UN in 1984 to 1985 and Desert Storm in 1990 to 1991. Otherwise, Greg considered himself a Cold War Marine. Greg retired in October 1991 as a lieutenant colonel. A 1967 graduate of Groton High School.

Greg Von Wald

131. **Robert A. Voss**, US Marines, 1970 Bristol High School graduate.

132. **Terry Walter**, Specialist 4, US Army, 2nd Infantry Division, 37th Field Artillery, South Korea. Served from 1972 through 1974. A 1968 Groton High School graduate and son of Mr. and Mrs. Vernon Walter of Groton.

133. **Robert Wegner**, US Army, Captain, in April 1973, participated in the annual spring field training exercise being held at Lake Poinsett, South Dakota. In April 1974, he graduated from the Army ROTC Flight Instruction Program at South Dakota State University. Helicopter Pilot, 3/5 Cavalry, Fort Lewis, Washington, from 1974 through 1979. A 1969 graduate of Groton High School.

Robert Wegner

134. **Lynn Weismantel,** US Army, Military Police, 1970 through 1972. 1968 graduate of Groton High School.

135. **Alvin Don Wellman,** US Army, joined in 1974 and discharged in 1976. Stationed in Germany. Family moved to Andover, and he attended Groton High School.

Lynn Weismantel

136. **Dale Wolter,** US Army, served in November 1963 through December 1964. A 1959 graduate of Groton High School.

Dale Wolter

137. **LeRoy Woods**, US Army, served in 1960 through 1963. Helicopter mechanic stationed in Europe for most of his service. Resident of Groton Care & Rehab Center for one year prior to his death.

138. **Roger E. Zastrow,** US Air Force, Airman, in October 1968, completed basic training at Lackland Air Force Base, Texas. Zastrow was stationed at Davis Monthan Air Force Base in Tucson, Arizona, where he was a

military pay specialist until his honorable discharge in 1970. Zastrow is a 1967 graduate of Groton High School and son of Mr. and Mrs. Alvin Zastrow of Columbia.

139. **Bob Zimney**, US Army. 1969 Groton High School graduate.

140. **Larry Zoellner,** US Army, Warrant Officer-Helicopter Pilot. Larry joined the US Army to learn to fly helicopters. He flew Bell AH-1 Cobra helicopters during his four years in the Army. During his life, he amassed almost 20,000 hours of flight experience in helicopter and fixed wing aircraft. After being discharged from the Army, he continued flying for different companies putting out forest fires among other things. He also started a tree nursery and grew Christmas trees. One of his hobbies was hang-gliding. He died in a freak hang-gliding accident in November 2000. Larry and his wife Danielle have two daughters, four grandchildren, and two great-grandchildren.

POW
Douglas Hegdahl—the Incredibly Stupid One

While researching the Vietnam conflict, I discovered an interesting story about a Douglas Hegdahl from Clark. He was born in 1946. I assume he graduated from Clark High School and joined the US Navy in 1965. After boot camp in San Diego, California, he was assigned to the USS *Canberra* (as a gunners-mate), a missile cruiser positioned in the Gulf of Tonkin, three miles off the coast of Vietnam. On April 6, 1967, he was knocked overboard by a blast from the ship's guns. For some reason he was not reported missing for two days. He was then assumed to be dead, and the crew held a memorial service. What was not known, was that Hegdahl had floated for 12 hours until a Cambodian fisherman found him and brought him to shore. He was then turned over to Vietnamese militiamen and subsequently taken to Hoa Lo Prison, more affectionately known as the Hanoi Hilton. The interrogators at the Hanoi Hilton did not believe Hegdahl's story and assumed he was a CIA agent. When he was instructed to write anti-war statements against the US, he agreed but pretended to be unable to read or write. He was assigned a teacher, but he appeared to be incapable of learning. The captors called him "the incredibly stupid one," deemed him non-threatening, and he was given pretty much the run of the entire camp. During his

Douglas Hegdahl

time at the Hanoi Hilton, he was given the task of sweeping the prison grounds. When no one was looking, he filled five army trucks' gas tanks with dirt and leaves so they would not operate. He would also take advantage of his freedom within the camp, often passing notes and communicating with other prisoners as he swept. The most amazing accomplishment, however, was his ability to memorize the names of prisoners, the date they were captured, the dates they arrived at the prison as well as other personal information, such as dog's name, kid's name, Social Security number, etc. Using the nursery rhyme "Old McDonald Had a Farm" as a mnemonic device, he memorized over 250 names. When the Vietnamese decided to release three prisoners from the camp, Hegdahl did not want to go. The soldiers had made a "No Go Home Early" pact in which they agreed that they would all go home together or not at all. Hegdahl was ordered by his commanding officer to return home to share the valuable information he had acquired at the Hanoi Hilton and was released with two other prisoners on August 5, 1969. He had been in captivity for 852 days. Back in the US, Hegdahl provided names of military and intelligence personnel who were thought to be deceased. His global impact came when he confronted the Vietnamese at the Paris Peace talks in 1970 after having been flown to Paris by Ross Perot. The information Hegdahl provided, including the locations and horrible conditions of the prison camps, as well as the torture practices used by the Vietnamese, were finally shared with the world. Exposing the Vietnamese this way may have led them to keep the prisoners alive until the conflict was over, potentially saving hundreds of prisoners. Not bad for a kid from Clark, South Dakota, deemed "the incredibly stupid one." Hegdahl received an honorable discharge from the US Navy in 1970 and remained in the inactive reserve until October 1972. He later had an outstanding career with the US Navy SERE School, teaching escape, evasion, and survival techniques to Navy personnel. For his service as a prisoner of war, Hegdahl was nominated for the following medals: Navy & Marine Corps Medal, Bronze Star Medal (with Valor Device), the Meritorious Service Medal, and the Navy Commendation Medal (with Valor Device). The Navy never approved any of these awards. This sounds a bit curious. Sounds like there might be something missing from the reports I read to complete this discussion.

Before I continue with my discussion of other military participation by area individuals, let me provide a narrative from Lieutenant General Harold G. Moore (Ret) concerning the Vietnam conflict. You might know this name if you read his book, *We Were Soldiers Once . . . And Young* or happened to see the movie directed and starred in by Mel Gibson by the same name. While the movie takes a lot of liberty in the actual events, it does give you an idea of not only the futility of war but the impact of fighting a war managed by numbers and politicians.

> "This story is about time and memories. The time was 1965, a different kind of war; a watershed year when one era was ending in America, and another was beginning. We felt it then, in the many ways our lives changed so suddenly, so dramatically, and looking back on it from a quarter-century gone, we are left in no doubt. It was the year America decided to directly intervene in the Byzantine affairs of obscure

and distant Vietnam. It was the year we went to war. In the broad, traditional sense, that 'we' who went to war was all of us, all Americans, though in truth at that time the larger majority had little knowledge of, less interest in, and no great concern with what was beginning so far away. So, this story is about the smaller, more tightly focused 'we' of that sentence; the first American combat troops who boarded WWII era troopships, sailed to that little-known place, and fought the first major battle of a conflict that would drag on for 10 long years and come as near to destroying America as it did to destroy Vietnam. The Ia Drang campaign was to the Vietnam War what the terrible Spanish Civil War of the 1930s was to WWII, a dress rehearsal; the place where new tactics, techniques, and weapons were tested, perfected, and validated.

In Ia Drang, both sides claimed victory and both sides drew lessons, some of them dangerously deceptive, which echoed and resonated throughout the decade of bloody fighting and bitter sacrifice that was to come. This is about what we did, what we say, what we suffered in the 34-day campaign in the Ia Drang Valley of the Central Highlands of South Vietnam in November 1965, when we were young, confident, and patriotic and our countrymen knew little and cared less about our sacrifices. We were the children of the 1950s, and we went where we were sent because we loved our country. We were draftees, most of us, but we were proud of the opportunity to serve that country just as our fathers had served in WWII and our older brothers in Korea. We went to war because our country asked us to go, because our new president, Lyndon Johnson, ordered us to go, but more importantly because we saw it as our duty to go. We were the children of the 1950s and John F. Kennedy's young stalwarts of the early 1960s. He told the world that Americans would 'pay any price, bear any burden, meet any hardship' in the defense of freedom. We were the down payment on that costly contract, but the man who signed it was not there when we fulfilled his promise.

John F. Kennedy waited for us on a hill in Arlington National Cemetery, and in time we came by the thousands to fill those slopes with our white marble markers and to ask on the murmur of the wind if that was truly the future we had envisioned for us. Among us were old veterans, grizzled sergeants who had fought in Europe and the Pacific in WWII and had survived the frozen hell of Korea, and now were about to add another star to their Combat Infantry Badge. There were regular army enlistees, young men from America's small towns whose fathers told them they would learn discipline and become real men in the Army. There were other young men who chose the Army over an equal term in prison. Alternative sentencing, the judges call it now. But the majority were draftees, 19- and 20-year-old boys summoned from across America by their local Selection Service Boards to do their two years in green. The PFC's (private first class) soldiered for $99.37 a month; the sergeants first class for $343.50 a month. Leading us were the sons of West Point and the young ROTC lieutenants from Rutgers and The Citadel, and yes, even Yale University, who had heard Kennedy's call and answered it. There were also the young, enlisted men and NCO's (noncommissioned officers) who passed through Officer Candidate School (OCS) and emerged newly minted officers and gentlemen. All laughed nervously when confronted with the cold statistics that measured a second lieutenant's combat life expectancy in minutes and seconds, not hours. Our second lieutenants were paid $241.20 per month.

The class of 1965 came out of the old America, a nation that disappeared forever in the smoke that billowed off the jungle battlegrounds where we fought and bled. The country that sent us off to war was not there to welcome us home. It no longer existed.

We answered the call of one president who was now dead; we followed the orders of another who would be hounded from office and haunted, by the war he mismanaged so badly. Many of our countrymen came to hate the war we fought. Those who hated it the most—the professionally sensitive—were not, in the end, sensitive enough to differentiate between the war and the soldiers who had been ordered to fight it. They hated us as well, and we went to ground in the crossfire, as we had learned in the jungles. In time our battles were forgotten, our sacrifices were discounted and both our sanity and our suitability for life in polite American society were publicly questioned. Our young-old faces, chiseled and gaunt from the fever and the heat and the sleepless nights, now stare back to us, lost and damned strangers, frozen in yellowing snapshots packed away in cardboard boxes with our medals and ribbons. We rebuilt our lives, found jobs or professions, married, raised families, and waited patiently for American to come to its senses. As the years passed, we search each other out and found that the half-remembered pride of service was shared by those who had shared everything else with us. With them, and only them, could we talk about what had really happened over there—what we had seen, what we had done, and what we had survived."

I realize this is long and I have reduced some of it, but it needs to be read in connection with my discussion of men and women who served in South Vietnam as well as those who volunteered to serve but did so outside of South Vietnam. Each of them came home to a dramatically different country.

As Lieutenant General Moore said, most of the fighting in any war is done by the kid from small town America. The officers are those from OCS, ROTC, or service academies. Groton and the surrounding area have historically given their sons to the needs of the country and done so during WWI, WWII, Korean War, and finally the Vietnam conflict. Brown County has had 130 war casualties. As you would expect, almost half died during the Second World War (64); 49 died during the First World War; four in the Korean War; and as previously discussed, 13 during Vietnam.

I have broken down the following area veteran participation in these wars and conflicts (from 1940 through 1961) by years and conflict. Information is based upon what is available from obituaries and personal knowledge. I am hopeful it is correct. I apologize for missing items and hope in the future that this can become a living document. Facts and circumstances will be updated as more and more friends, relatives, etc. provide me additional information. Typical of all war veterans, most of these individuals came home and went back to their families and jobs. Some to colleges. Few discussed the wars. They mourned by themselves. Most of their accomplishments and service remained to themselves until they died, and we read their obituaries. It's time we should gather such information and be proud of what they did for us.

WWII—KOREA FROM 1940 THROUGH 1955

1. **Alvin T. Abeln,** US Army, 2nd Lieutenant, in July 1955, graduated from the motor transportation course at the Infantry School at Fort Benning, Georgia. Abeln is a 1950 graduate of Groton High School and a 1954 graduate of South Dakota State College. Husband of Loretta and son of Mrs. Vera B. Abeln of Groton.

   Alvin T. Abeln

2. **Clarence Abeln,** US Navy, commander of a flight training squadron and later served two years in the Bureau of Aeronautics in Washington DC. Born in Groton and son of Joe and Elisabeth Abeln. Uncle of Alvin and Eugene Abeln.

3. **Eugene Abeln,** US Marines, served from 1946 through 1948.

4. **Arthur R. Adler,** US Navy, Seaman Apprentice, in April 1951, was stationed aboard *Tobias ABVA*, an aircraft repair ship. Son of Mr. and Mrs. Arthur Adler Sr. of Groton. 1948 graduate of Groton High School.

   Eugene Abeln

5. **Charles Lavern Ahern,** US Air Force, made a career of the Air Force and retired in Denver in 1969. Graduated

from Groton High School in 1943 and raised on a farm near Andover.

6. **Walter (Wally) Adler,** US Army, entered Army in 1954 and discharged in 1956. Graduated from Groton High School in 1952.

7. **Warren F. Ahern,** US Navy, Airman Apprentice in 1951. Reported for duty in March 1951 for advanced training at the US Naval Air Station, Corpus Christi, Texas. A 1948 graduate of Groton High School.

8. **George Alberts, Jr.,** US Air Force, weatherman and accomplished sharpshooter, entered the Air Force in 1944 and was discharged October 1946. A 1944 graduate of Groton High School.

George Alberts, Jr.

9. **Kenneth Alberts,** served in WWII.

10. **Norman L. Anderson,** US Navy, served 20 years, deployed in the West Pacific, Korea, Vietnam, and the Marshall Islands during the atomic bomb testing. Awarded several medals, including National Defense Service Medal, Good Conduct Medal, Vietnam Service Medal, and Navy Unit Commendation. Attended country schools in the Pierpont area. Later in life, Anderson moved to Groton.

11. **Robert Anderson**, US Navy, enlisted in 1944 and discharged 1946. Assigned to the battleship USS *New Mexico*. Spent a year in the Pacific area taking part in the landing at Luzon on January 6, 1945, when the ship was hit by a suicide plane. The ship was hit again

at Okinawa and a third time, which killed 56 men on board. Anderson returned to Andover following his discharge and died in 2008.

12. **Nichlos Arndt,** US Army, served during the Korean War, discharged in 1953. Graduated from Groton High School in 1951 and was Governor of Boys State in 1950.

13. **Kenneth V. Ascher,** served during WWII. Moved to Groton in 1982 when he retired.

14. **Oren Ausland,** US Army, Corporal, served 1944–1946, native of Andover. Received two battle stars, Asiatic and Pacific Theater and Philippines Ribbon.

Oren Ausland

15. **Hal J. Babbe,** US Army, 2nd Lieutenant, in January 1954, took an 11-week, basic infantry officer's course at Fort Benning, Georgia. In September 1954, Babbe was assigned to the 10th Infantry Division at Fort Riley, Kansas. Entered military in September 1953. Son of G.J. Babbe of Turton.

16. **Arthur Bahr**, US Army, Korea 1953.

17. **James Baldry,** US Army and US Navy. Enlisted in the US Navy in 1942 and served on an aircraft carrier a Bougainville. At the end of his enlistment in the Navy, he joined the US Army and served for 24 years prior to his retirement in 1969. He was the recipient of six battle stars, two Oak Leaf Clusters, and Silver Star. Baldry was born in Groton and graduated from Groton High School in 1940.

18. **Lewis Barondeau,** US Army, WWII, Normandy on D-Day with the 35th Infantry Division, where he was a driver and mechanic. Resident of Conde.

19. **Gerald LeRoy Barrie,** US Navy, Ship Serviceman Second Class, in September 1956, reported aboard the Naval Field, Corpus Christi, Texas. Entered the Navy in April 1945. Was assigned to Pearl Harbor, then assigned to aircraft carrier, USS *Philippine Sea* based at San Diego, California. Son of Mr. and Mrs. Lawrence Barrie of Turton.

20. **Kenneth D. Barrie,** US Air Force, Airman First Class, in December 1955, was on a 25-day furlough with his parents, Mr. and Mrs. Lawrence Barrie of Turton. Spent a year at Sidi Simane Air Force Base in French Morocco, and the balance of his enlistment was at Campbell Air Force Base, Kentucky.

21. **Rolland Barrie,** US Air Force, in April 1956, returned to Spokane, Washington, after a 30-day furlough with his parents, Mr. and Mrs. Armond Barrie of Turton.

22. **Charles Barthle,** US Army, Colonel (Ret). Served as a signal officer maintaining communications for General Patton during WWII. Taught at West Point. Worked with Dr. Von Braun at Redstone Arsenal, starting up the Army Ballistic Missile Agency. Born in Groton in 1917 and graduated from Groton High School in 1936. Received a Bachelor of Science from South Dakota State University in 1941 and a master's degree in electrical engineering from the University of Illinois.

23. **Boyd Barwin,** US Air Force, Military Police. Enlisted in Air Force in 1949. After retirement, Barwin came to South Dakota and married his high school sweetheart, Diane Gibbs-Paul, in 2000 and lived in Groton.

24. **Lyman Fiske Bates,** US Navy, Aviator, completed instruction in fighter planes and later flew transports to the Pacific Theater. After being discharged from the service, he eventually went to work with Standard Oil where his first assignment was in Groton. Member of the Masonic Lodge in Groton for more than 50 years.

25. **Glenn Baule,** US Navy, WWII, native of Andover.

26. **William Baule,** US Army, served for 18 months as military police in Germany. Native of Andover.

27. **Otis M. Belden**, US Navy, served in 1945 and 1946. Radarman 3rd Class, served aboard the amphibious flagship USS *Mount Olympus* in the Pacific Theater. Belden was in Tokyo Bay on September 2, 1945, when Japan surrendered. After the surrender, the ship ferried occupation troops around the Far East. In addition, they also collected Japanese arms and dumped them at sea. A 1939 graduate of Groton High School.

Otis Belden

28. **Thomas Benda,** US Army, served from 1945 through 1947 and from 1951 to 1954, Korean War.

29. **Robert G. Benson,** US Army, served during WWII. Graduated from Groton

Thomas Benda

High School in 1940. Brother of Joyce Sundling of Groton.

30. **Bobby O. Berg,** US Marines, Private First Class, in January 1959, served with Second Battalion, 1st Marine Division and rotated to Okinawa, Japan. Son of Mr. and Mrs. Joe Berg of Andover.

31. **Donald M. Berreth,** US Navy, in July 1953, left for basic training in Great Lakes, Illinois. Son of Mr. and Mrs. Ernest Berreth of Groton. A 1953 graduate of Groton High School.

32. **Robert Bingen,** US Army, Private, in March 1952 furloughed to visit his mother, Mrs. Lillian Bingen of Andover.

33. **Darrel Ray Bingham,** US Navy, enlisted in 1944 and discharged in 1949. Born in Groton and graduated from Groton High School in 1943.

34. **James D. Blair,** US Army, served during the years 1955-1956. Born in Webster and raised in the Groton/Andover area and attended Groton High School.

35. **John Blair,** US Air Force, Airman 1st Class, enlisted in 1950 and served until 1954. Served overseas on Okinawa during the Korean War. Attended grade school at the Groton Township School and two years of high school at Groton High School. Sixty-year member of the American Legion.

36. **Thomas (Chick) Blair**, US Army, enlisted October 1941 and served in England, France, and Belgium. Was in the Battle of the Bulge during Christmas of 1944 and was wounded at Remagen Ridge. He was discharged in November 1945. Graduated from Groton High School.

Chick and Lyle Blair

37. **Lyle Blair,** veteran of WWII. Past post commander and past county commander of the American Legion and was also a past Legion state officer. Graduate of Groton High School.

38. **Jeannette Blader Reid,** US Navy Wave, 1940 Groton High School graduate. Enlisted in 1943 and discharged in 1946.

Jeanette Blader Reid

39. **Walter Blondo,** US Army, served during WWII in the European Theater. Moved to Groton in 1970 when Blondo and his wife, Myrtle Marie, owned and operated the Wheel Inn Café and Grocery in Ferney.

40. **Wilbur W. Bohling,** US Air Force, Private in 1951. Son of Mr. and Mrs. Henry Bohling of Columbia. Was an Air Force technician.

41. **Don Bowles,** US Army, Lieutenant Colonel, called to active duty in the Quarter Master Corps. He was promoted to captain in 1942 and Lieutenant Colonel

in 1943. On December 10, 1944, the 70th Infantry Division arrived in Marseilles, France. He was director of the Quarter Master Corps for that division. His division engaged the German 6th Mountain Division of S.S. Troops in the Battle of the Bulge on Christmas Eve 1944. Don received the Bronze Star and was discharged in 1945. He and his brother-in-law, Dale Sour, purchased the Groton Ford dealership from Don's father. Bowles was born in Groton and graduated from Groton High School in 1932. Graduated from South Dakota State University with a degree in electrical engineering in 1936.

42. **Alfred Breitkreutz**, US Air Force, Captain. Entered the Air Force in 1946 and was shot down and killed in Korea by a MIG in June 1952. He held the Distinguished Flying Cross and Air Medal with seven Oak Leaf Clusters. The son of Mr. and Mrs. Alfred Breitkreutz of Groton.

43. **Harold Brekke,** US Army, Technician Third Grade, served from 1942 through 1944, native of Andover. Served in the Panama Canal Zone. Good Conduct Medal.

Harold Brekke

44. **Roland Brooks,** US Army, Captain, WWI and WWII. Moved to Groton in the 1950s where he was a real estate and insurance agent until retirement.

45. **Bill Brotherton,** US Army, served during WWII in the South Pacific and Japan.

Bill Brotherton

Elected to the Groton City Council in 1993 and served until his death in 2005.

46. **Blaine E. Buntrock,** US Army, Private First Class, entered the Army in February 1954. In July 1955, Buntrock was a member of the 24th Infantry Division in Korea. 1952 graduate of Columbia High School. Son of Mr. and Mrs. Ben H. Buntrock of Columbia.

47. **Dean Buntrock,** US Army, Private First Class, in October 1953, was assigned to Fort Leonard Wood, Missouri, as a member of the finance office. Son of Mr. and Mrs. Rudy Buntrock of Columbia.

48. **Ralph L. Buntrock,** US Navy, Hospital Corpsman 3rd Class, in March 1957, served aboard USS *Magoffin*, a unit of the 7th Fleet operating in the Far East. Was scheduled to return in May 1957. Son of Mr. and Mrs. Ben H. Buntrock of Columbia. Husband of the former Margie A. Pence of Columbia.

49. **Walter Buntrock,** US Navy, Seaman First Class, served from 1942 through 1945 South West Pacific Theater, native of Columbia. Received Guam and Leyte Battle Stars.

Walter Buntrock

50. **Ronald J. Bymers,** US Army, in December 1953, was assigned to Camp Kilmer, New Jersey, from where he was assigned to Germany. Native of Verdon.

51. **John S. Carr,** US Army, Private First Class, in September 1952, completed basic training and leadership course in the Hawaii Islands. Later assumed instructor duties in Fort Custer, Michigan. Son of Mr. and Mrs. John Carr of Andover.

52. **Carl Carlson,** US Army, Private, August through December 1945, native of Columbia.

53. **Edwin Carlson,** US Navy, enlisted in 1942 and served three years with the Seabees in the Philippines. When he left the Navy, he concentrated on his education and family and later a successful career as an engineer and businessman in Arizona. He passed away in 2004. Originally from Columbia.

Edwin Carlson

54. **Henry Carlson,** US Army, Platoon Sergeant, brother of Edwin Carlson, also from Columbia. Henry was wounded in the Pacific and recuperated at a rehabilitation camp near Clark Field Air Base on Luzon. Henry died in 1996. Received Asia Pacific Theater Campaign, WWII Victory, and Army of Occupation WWII.

Henry Carlson

55. **Donald H. Cassels,** US Army, Private First Class, in December 1955, was awarded the Good Conduct Medal in Germany while serving with the Service Battery of the 1st Infantry Division as a truck driver. A 1954 graduate of Groton High School. Entered the Army in February 1954 and arrived in Germany the following August. Son of Mrs. Martha Cassels of Groton.

56. **Gordon J. Cavanaugh,** US Navy, Metalsmith Second Class, in June 1952, graduated from US Naval Welding School, Great Lakes, Illinois. In October 1956, Cavanaugh was assigned to the 40th Field Maintenance Squadron at Smokey Hill Air Force Base, Salina, Kansas. Son of Pearl Cavanaugh of Andover.

57. **John M. Clark,** US Air Force, Airman Second Class, in October 1955, was a member of the air crew that was named "engineering crew of the month" in the Japan-based 56th Weather Reconnaissance Squadron. Clark graduated from Groton High School in 1950 and entered the Air Force in December 1952. Son of Mr. and Mrs. John L. Clark of Groton.

John M. Clark

58. **Luverne Clark,** Master Sergeant (Ret), Hecla, served in WWII, Korea (twice), and Vietnam. Awarded Bronze Star, Army Commendation Medal/2 Oak Leaf Cluster and Vietnam Service.

Luverne Clark

59. **Carroll Clocksene**, US Navy, served in 1953 through 1957. Dispersing clerk stationed at Corpus Christi, Texas for two and a half years. In November 1955, Clocksene was on furlough with his parents, Mr. and Mrs. Lyle Clocksene of Groton. Subsequently assigned to duty in Guam. A 1951 graduate of Groton High School.

Carroll Clocksene

60. **Robert C. Cook,** US Army, entered the Army in 1939. WWII veteran. Graduated from Groton High School.

61. **Dwayne Coon**, US Air Force, Airman 2nd Class, served from 1954 through 1958. Stationed in Cheyenne, Wyoming, Labrador, Newfoundland, and Peoria, Illinois.

62. **Dale W. Cooper,** US Army, Private, in October 1954, arrived in Korea for duty with the 807th Army Unit. Cooper, an engineer equipment repairman, entered the Army in February 1954. Son of Mr. and Mrs. James W. Cooper of Groton. A 1952 graduate of Groton High School.

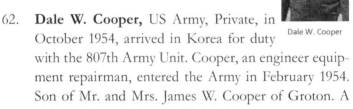

Dale W. Cooper

63. **Claire R. Cowen,** US Air Force, in September 1952, was assigned to Camp Stoneman, California, to disembark to the Far East as senior communications specialist. Wife and daughter made their home in Verdon while overseas. Graduated from Groton High School in 1948.

Claire R. Cowen

64. **Dana C. Craig,** US Navy, enlisted after he graduated from Groton High School in 1939.

65. **Donald "Bud" Craig,** US Army, Staff Sergeant, European Theater and Battle of the Bulge. He entered the Army after graduation from Groton High School in 1939 and was called back into the service when WWII started. Awarded a sharpshooter medal and an expert bayonet medal.

Bud Craig

66. **Lyle Cutler,** US Army, Corporal, was assigned to 557th Engineer Technical Intelligence Team, stationed in Korea all of 1953. Native of Claremont.

67. **Verl Cutler,** US Navy, Yeoman Third Class, discharged in 1946. Native of Claremont.

68. **Wayne Cutler,** US Army, medic in Antwerp, Belgium. Graduated from Claremont High School.

69. **Jerome Dale,** US Army, enlisted in 1944 and served in WWII in Saipan. Graduated from Lilly High School in 1943. Resident of Groton when he passed away.

70. **Edward J. Daly,** US Army, enlisted in Army in 1942 and was discharged January 1946. Graduated from Columbia High School in 1942.

71. **Daryl K. Danielson,** US Air Force, served during Korean War. Married to Ardis Schuelke, and after discharge, Danielson worked for the Groton Ford dealership.

72. **Dale Dayton,** US Army, enlisted in May 1945 and served in Pacific Theater. Discharged December 1946. Born near Stratford and graduated from Stratford High School in 1942.

73. **Carroll Dean,** US Army, attempted to enlist three times. On third attempt, Dean became member of the Army, even with suspect eyesight. Heavy weapons specialist, but war ended before Dean could utilize the training. Spent his enlistment in France near Paris. Was able to see Germany, Belgium, France, and Switzerland

while stationed in Europe after the war ended. Returned to Wisconsin. After trade school, Dean came to South Dakota, met his wife (married 69 years as of December 2020) and lived in Columbia and Groton.

74. **Burdette Denholm,** US Army, Specialist, served from 1954 through 1956, served in Panama, and native of Andover.

75. **Robert Denholm,** US Marines, served 1938 through 1939 and 1942 through 1945, served in the Pacific Theater of Operations. Native of Andover.

Robert Denholm

76. **Allan P. Dennert,** US Air Force, in April 1953 completed basic training at Lackland Air Force Base, Texas. Son of Mr. and Mrs. Robert H. Dennert of Columbia. Graduated from Columbia High School in 1949.

77. **Lloyd Dennert,** US Army, Private First Class in 1951, from Columbia. Completed training at Francis E. Warren Air Force Base near Cheyenne, Wyoming.

78. **Donald W. DeVries,** US Army, Private, in December 1956, received advanced infantry training with the 4th Division, Fort Lewis, Washington. A 1950 graduate of Pierpont High School and son of Mr. and Mrs. Thomas DeVries of Andover.

79. **James L. DeVries,** US Air Force, in September 1952, trained as an Air Force technician at Warren Air Base, Wyoming. Son of Mr. Thomas DeVries of Andover.

80. **Warren Dittus**, US Army, served from 1945 through 1946.

81. **Emil H. Dobberpfuhl,** US Air Force, Major. In August 1951, Dobberpfuhl was promoted from enlisted man to major after 25 years of service, native of Groton.

82. **Eugene E. Dobberphuhl,** US Air Force, in June 1952, was assigned to training as Air Force technician at the US Air Force Technical School at Warren Air Base, Wyoming. Son of Mrs. Edwin Dobberphuhl of Verdon. A 1951 graduate of Groton High School.

Bob McFarlane, Gene Dobberphuhl, Ken Hoops

83. **Francis Dohman,** US Marines, Pacific Theatre. Member of Carlson Raiders, 2nd Raider Battalion. The first US special operations force to form and see combat duty in WWII. Light infantry and special operations, and counterterrorism.

84. **Leslie Dohman,** US Army, Korea.

85. **LeRoy Dohrman,** US Army, Private, in February 1956, reported to duty at Fort Riley, Kansas, after a 30-day furlough with mother, Alvina Dohrman of Andover.

Les Dohman

86. **Manley Dohrman,** US Army, Private First Class, in April 1956, became a member of the 1st Infantry Division at Fort Riley, Kansas, as a machine gunner in Company H, 26th Regiment. Previously served in Iceland. Entered the Army in October 1953. Graduated from Langford High School in 1950. Son of Mrs. Alvina Dohrman of Andover.

87. **Leslie Dokter,** US Marines, Master Sergeant, was discharged from the US Air Force in June 1953 as chief master sergeant, then appointed as a master sergeant in the US Marines assigned to an air unit after completion of basic training. Dokter is from Andover and son of Mr. and Mrs. John Dokter of Andover.

88. **Ralph S. Dokter,** US Navy, in 1951, served aboard USS *Seminole* which participated in the invasion of Inchon and Wousan, Korea. Native of Andover.

89. **Donald E. Dombrowe,** US Navy, 12 years of service during WWII and the Korean W. A Pearl Harbor survivor. Born in Groton and married Anna Marie Bahr in 1949 in Groton.

90. **Harvey Dorfschmidt,** US Navy, a 1944 graduate of Groton High School.

91. **Lester Drager,** US Marines, joined in June 1946 and served in the Asiatic Pacific area. Retired in Groton in 1991.

Harvey Dorfschmidt

92. **Dale Dunker**, US Navy, drafted into the Navy in 1945. Stationed in Guam and assigned to an aircraft carrier in preparation of the expected invasion of Japan. After the Japanese surrender, Dale was honorably discharged in 1946. A 1939 graduate of Groton High School.

93. **Wallace Dunker,** US Army, enlisted in 1943. Served in the European Theater of Operations in WWII starting in 1943 and was discharged in 1946.

Wallace and Dale Dunker

Graduated from Groton High School in 1938. Brother of Dale Dunker.

94. **Jerry Dunn,** US Navy, in September 1956, received his discharge from the US Navy after serving four years. Dunn and his mother, Julia Dunn, made their home in California. Dunn was a native of Turton.

95. **William J. Dunn,** US Navy, in February 1951, was assigned to Navy Great Lakes, Illinois. A native of Turton.

96. **Donald Easterby,** US Army, Private First Class, in February 1951 was a specialized B-36 mechanic and assigned to Travis Air Force Base, CA. Son of Mr. and Mrs. Silas Easterby of Andover.

97. **Gerald A. Easterby,** US Army, Private, in July 1953, spent a 30-day furlough with his parents, after being assigned to Fort Baker, CA, for military police training. Stationed near Los Angeles, California. Shortly after returning from Korea in February 1955, Easterby received his discharge from the Army. Son of Mr. and Mrs. Silas Easterby of Andover.

98. **Elmo L. Ellingson,** US Army, enlisted in December 1953, native of Stratford.

99. **Lyle C. Ellingson,** US Army, Private, in October 1954, began eight-week basic training at the Anti-Aircraft Artillery Replacement Training Center, Fort Bliss, Texas. In December 1955, Ellingson was assigned to the aggressor force in Exercise Sage Brush underway in Louisiana. His wife, Mary Ann, and son, Terry, lived

in Aberdeen during the exercise. Son of Mr. and Mrs. Carl Ellingson of Stratford.

100. **Russell J. Ellingson,** US Army, reported for a physical in August 1951, native of Groton.

101. **Harlan E. Ellis,** US Navy, Seaman Apprentice, in September 1956, completed basic training at Great Lakes, Illinois Naval Training Station. At the expiration of leave, he reported to Great Lakes Training Station for additional training. Son of Mr. and Mrs. Cyril Ellis of Columbia.

102. **Dean Emmen,** US Air Force, in February 1959, completed basic training in Texas. Son of Mr. and Mrs. Hans Emmen of Andover.

103. **Erwin G. Emmen,** US Army, PFC, served from April 1942 until September 1945. Served 26 months overseas in Sicily, Naples-Foggia, Rome-Arno, Southern France, Rhineland, and Central Europe as a truck driver. He drove, maintained, and performed first echelon maintenance on all Army vehicles up to and including two-and-half-ton trucks. Hauled ammunition and demolition materials and drove in convoys under blackout conditions over rough terrain. He was awarded Bronze Arrowhead, Bronze Medal, and Purple Heart. He didn't talk about his military days much, only that he wanted nothing to do with the Germans and Italians. After his discharge from the Army, he married and lived in the Andover area, farming land northeast of Andover. Erwin was born in January 1920 to George and Emma Emmen of Andover and died in March 1975. He is

buried in the Andover Cemetery. Dean Emmen, above, is Erwin's nephew.

104. **Donald Engstrom,** US Navy, Photographer's Mate, 3rd Class. Formerly a native of Andover.

105. **Jerroll Erdmann,** US Air Force, enlisted in 1952 and stationed at Gary Air Force Base in San Marcos, Texas, where he worked as a helicopter mechanic during the Korean War. Erdmann was discharged in 1956. Graduated from Groton High School in 1950.

106. **Lynn Erdmann,** US Army, Sergeant, served in 1942 through 1945, European Theater of Operations. Awarded Silver Star, Bronze Star, and European Theater with 4 stars. Hometown is Stratford, South Dakota.

Lynn Erdmann

Marvin Erdman

107. **Marvin Erdman,** US Navy, a 1936 graduate of Groton High School.

108. **Richard Erdmann,** US Navy, Electrician's Mate, served from 1942 through 1945, Atlantic and Pacific Theaters, native of Stratford.

109. **Clarence Erickson,** US Navy, Seaman First Class, served from 1944 through 1946 in Asia Pacific Theatre of Operations and was awarded Asia Pacific Victory medals. Native of Groton.

Clarence Erickson

110. **Myron Erickson,** US Navy, served in the South Pacific during WWII aboard the US *Oahu*. Resident of Groton at the time of his death in 1985.

111. **Al Face,** US Army, First Lieutenant, served from 1941 through 1943 in Caribbean, native of Stratford.

Myron Erickson

112. **Eugene L. Face,** US Air Force, Staff Sergeant, in April 1953, completed basic training at Lackland Air Force Base, Texas. Served 1953-1957. Awarded National Defense Service and Korean Service medals. Son of Mr. and Mrs. George Face of Stratford.

Eugene Face

113. **Knolen Face,** US Navy, Private, served from 1944 through 1945 in American Expeditionary Forces, and he is a native of Stratford.

114. **Wesley L. Face,** US Army, Corporal, in March 1952, graduated with honors from Technical Mechanical Training School at Chanute Air Force Base, Illinois. Became an instructor. Entered service in August 1951 and is a graduate of Northern State Teachers College. Son of Mr. and Mrs. Lloyd Face of Stratford.

Knolen Face

115. **Mark Falknor,** US Army, Signal Corps, served in the European Theater until the end of WWII. Attended Groton schools and farmed with his father in the Groton area.

116. **James (Jim) Feist,** no information available.

117. **Frank Felix,** US Army, graduated from Columbia High School in 1948.

118. **Mike Felix,** US Navy, Seaman First Class, served from 1944 through 1946, native of Columbia, received Asiatic and Pacific Ribbons.

Mike Felix

119. **Alvin C. Feller Jr.,** US Army Air Force, Captain, in July 1942, was drafted and stationed at McChord Airfield in Tacoma, Washington. Attended Officer Candidate School and was stationed at Herington, Kansas, and Bolling Field, Washington DC. Discharged in August 1946 as a captain. Born on the Feller farm outside Groton.

120. **Delton S. Feller,** US Navy, served 20 years after enlisting in 1927. Graduated from Groton High School in 1927.

121. **Jason Feller,** service during WWII. Graduated from Groton High School in 1931.

122. **Donavon D. Fenske,** US Army, Private, native of Ferney, in January 1953, completed basic combat training at the Signal Corps Replacement Center at Camp Gordon, Georgia. Son of Mr. and Mrs. Ray Fenske of Aberdeen.

123. **Gordon Flemmer,** US Army, enlisted and served from 1946 through 1947. Served in the US Army of Occupation of Japan. Graduated from Selby High

School in 1943. Farmed in Andover after being discharged.

124. **Harvey Fliehs**, US Army, Corporal, truck Driver and interpreter, served in 1944 through 1946. Participated in D-Day landing at Utah Beach. Received three bronze service campaign stars.

Harvey Fliehs

125. **Irvin Fliehs**, US Army, March 1945, Fliehs entered the US Army. Discharged following the end of WWII. Graduated from Groton High School.

126. **Harold H. Fransen,** US Army, WWII. Formerly of Groton. Member of Emmanuel Lutheran Church and American Legion.

Irvin Fliehs

127. **Eddie L. Fredrickson,** veteran of WWII. Born in Verdon. Lived in Groton 25 years prior to his death in 1985.

128. **Frank Fryer,** veteran of WWII. Employed by Siefkes Truck Line in Groton prior to his death in 1968.

129. **Charles E. Fuller,** US Navy, 1st Class Seaman, killed in action on November 19, 1942. Fuller was born and raised in Groton and graduated from Groton High School in 1935.

130. **Raymond Fuller,** US Army, veteran of WWII. Born in Groton in 1913 and graduated from Groton High School in 1933.

131. **Henry Gabbert,** veteran of WWII. Gabert was born in Stratford in 1904. Lived in Verdon and Stratford his entire life.

132. **Allan Gerharter,** US Army, Corporal, enlisted in 1953 and served until discharged in 1955. Born in Groton in 1931 and graduated from Stratford High School.

133. **Clayton (Kelly) Gibbs,** US Army. Buried with military rites conducted by Groton Post No. 39. Died in 1978 and lived in Groton since 1929.

Kelly Gibbs

134. **John A. Gibbs,** veteran of WWII. Resident of Groton and passed away in February 1963.

135. **Charles E. Griffith,** US Air Force, Major, in March 1958 received his regular Air Force commission. Served in the Air Force reserve for the previous 15 years. Brother of Mrs. Stanley Dennert of Houghton, and former native of Houghton and Groton.

136. **Harlyn Grote,** US Army, entered service in October 1951 and shipped to Aberdeen Proving Grounds, base for all Army ordinance testing and development. Chose small arms training but was given Automotive Machine School instead. Most of his basic training company was shipped to Korea. Grote was shipped to Hanau, Germany, and assigned to the 587th Engineer Field Maintenance, a company of 87 men. Responsibility was to ensure that all machinery was ready to go to war with the East Germans or Russians. Graduated from

Aberdeen High School in 1948 and expected to celebrate his 70th wedding anniversary in December 2020. Member of American Legion, Groton.

137. **Ronald Gubin,** US Army, Private, served 1953 through 1956. Native of Stratford.

138. **Clifford Hall,** graduate of Columbia High School. Killed in action during WWII.

Ronald Gubin

139. **Rex Hammond,** US Navy, WWII, served in 1942 through 1945, South Pacific and Japan, graduate of Columbia High School.

140. **John L. Hanlon,** US Navy, 1944 through 1946, completed basic training in Idaho and joined the USS *Hilo* which contributed to the hard-fought Buna-Gona campaign in New Guinea. One of the first ships to be used as a motor torpedo boat tender. *Hilo's* task was to act in remote areas to help with gathering intelligence, assisting in the necessary fuel, ammunition, and provisions for the torpedo boats. Near the end of the war, the *Hilo* was used for transporting prisoners and personnel. In 1949, John married Dina Jerke in Webster, SD. They raised five children on a small farm south of Bath, SD. Dina passed away in 2002 and John in November 2013. "Information provided by his grandson, Josh Hanlon."

John L. Hanlon

141. **Harvey Hannon,** US Army, Private, in April 1954 left for Fort Lewis, Washington, for duty in the Pacific. Son of Mrs. Elsie Hannon of Andover. Graduated from Andover High School in 1949.

142. **George M. Hansen,** US Navy, Petty Officer Second Class, in February 1957, graduated from recruit training at the Great Lake Naval Training Center, Illinois. Son of Mr. and Mrs. George Hansen of Stratford. Served 1952-1963 with a final rank of petty office second class. Awarded the National Defense Service Medal.

George Hansen

143. **Robert Hanson,** US Air Force, graduated in 1948 from Columbia High School.

144. **Robert Harnois,** US Army Air Corps, WWII veteran. Graduated from Groton High School.

145. **Maurice Harry**, US Army, 1945.

146. **C. Darrel Haskell,** US Army, served in 1952 to 1954. Served in Germany, Headquarters Company, 169th Infantry Regiment. Graduated from Conde High School in 1949.

147. **George Healy,** US Army, 1953 graduate of Columbia High School.

148. **Michael P. Healy,** US Marines, Corporal, in December 1953, completed six months of training with the 1st Provisional Marine Air Ground Task Force in Hawaii. Graduated from Columbia High School in 1950 and married to Irene Buntrock of Columbia.

149. **Norbert Hearnen**, US Marines, Korea, served from 1950 through 1954. Graduated from Conde High School in 1950. Raised in the Turton area.

150. **Edwin Heidzig,** graduate of Columbia High School.

151. **Gary Heitmann,** US Air Force, enlisted after graduating from Britton High School and was also a reservist. Worked for the Schuring farms for 15 years.

Gary Heitmann

152. **Donald Hein,** US Army, Private, in January 1955, returned to Fort Bliss, Texas after spending a furlough with his parents, Mr. and Mrs. William Hein of Andover.

153. **Arthur Leon Helmer,** veteran of WWII. Graduated from Andover High School in 1943.

154. **Donald E. Helmer,** US Air Force, Colonel (Ret), in July 1953, received the wings of an Air Force pilot in ceremonies held at Webb Air Force Base, Texas. A jet pilot, Helmer was assigned to further training in gunnery tactics. In November 1953, Helmer left for California for overseas duty. In August 1955, he reported for duty at Clovis, New Mexico. Retired in 1984 with the 47th Flying Training Wing at Laughlin Air Force Base, Del Rio, Texas. Son of Mr. and Mrs. Henry Helmer of Andover.

155. **Orville Helmer,** in April 1953, was discharged after returning from Korea. Served in Korea for 18 months. Son of Mr. and Mrs. Henry Helmer of Andover. Graduated from Andover High School in 1947.

156. **Richard Helmer,** US Army Air Corps/Air Force, stationed in Philippines and the 20th Air Force Base in Guam as Motor Pool sergeant. Received the Asiatic

Pacific Service Medal and Victory Medal. Drafted in 1944 after graduating from Andover High School in 1944.

157. **Loren Hemen,** US Army, WWII veteran. Lived and worked in Columbia until moving to Jamestown, North Dakota.

158. **Dyle W. Henderson,** US Army, Combat Military Police, served in North Africa, Italy, France, and Germany. Born in Groton and graduated from Groton High School in 1936.

159. **Melvin Henjum,** US Army, enlisted after graduating from Conde High School and served during WWII from 1942 to 1945 in the European Theater.

160. **Milo L. Herman,** US Army, Corporal, in early 1951, was promoted to corporal at Ford Ord, California and discharged in November 1951. Son of Mr. and Mrs. Frank Herman of Columbia.

161. **Marx Herther,** US Navy, 1945-1947, graduate of Columbia High School, Columbia Volunteer Fire Chief for 10 years, Columbia Commercial Club, Columbia City Council, Columbia Alumni Association President, and participated in the organization of the 1965 all-class reunion, Columbia American Legion Adjutant, and other Legion offices over the years. Died in 1994 at age of 70 in Columbia.

Marx Herther

162. **Norman Herther,** US Army, 1943-1946, graduate of Hecla High School, former Columbia resident.

163. **Norman Hewitt,** US Navy, served from 1943 through 1946, served in South Pacific. Long-time Claremont farmer who was born and raised in Hecla.

Norman Herther

164. **Robert Hinderks,** US Navy, Yeoman Third Class, served from 1945 through 1946, Pacific and Atlantic areas of operation, native of Columbia.

165. **Rix R. Hinckley,** US Marine, served in the Korean War. Born in Groton and graduated from Aberdeen Central.

166. **Don Hinrichs**, US Navy, served from 1942 through 1946.

167. **Max V. Hinrichs,** WWII veteran. Resident of Claremont

168. **Maurice Hitchock**, US Army, Purple Heart recipient, served from 1943 through 1945, native of Conde.

169. **Jerome Hochhalter,** US Army, Private First Class, in January 1957, qualified as expert in firing the M-1 rifle at Fort Riley, Kansas. A jeep driver in Company C of the 1st Infantry Division's 18th Regiment. Entered the service in September 1955 and completed basic training at Fort Carson, Colorado. Son of Mr. and Mrs. Helmuth Hochhalter of Columbia.

Maurice Hitchcock

170. **William T. Holbert,** US Navy, in November 1953, received the Air Medal at ceremonies at the Alameda, California Naval Air Station. The air medal is presented to officers and men who have completed 20 or more combat flights. Son of Mr. and Mrs. Howard Holbert of Amherst.

171. **Jack Holcomb,** US Navy, Motor Machinist's Mate, South Pacific, served from 1942 through 1945, native of Stratford.

172. **Marvin Holcomb,** US Army, WWII veteran, served from 1942 through 1946. Born in Stratford.

Jack Holcomb

173. **Dale Holler** served in Korea with the 45th Division as a radio man. Son of Mr. and Mrs. Frank Holler of Andover.

174. **Dwaye Holler,** US Army, enlisted in December 1953. Son of Mr. and Mrs. Frank Holler of Andover.

175. **Dwayne Holler,** US Army, Corporal, Medical Corp, in 1952, returned from a 10-month tour in Korea.

Robert Hood

176. **Robert A. Hood,** US Army, 1st Lieutenant, reported for physical in October 1951. Served in Japan and Korea. In July 1953, a letter he had written home was read to the Brown County Rural Youth. A 1945 graduate of Groton High School.

177. **Clifford Hoops**, US Army/Air Force, Technical Sergeant, served from 1945 through 1946.

Clifford Hoops

James Hoops

178. **James Hoops,** US Army, served from 1945 through 1946, Asia Pacific Theater. Received Asia Pacific Theater Service and Victory medals. Native of Ferney.

179. **Kenny Hoops,** Air Force, served in Germany in the 1950s.

180. **Jerry Hoops,** US Army, served in the 1950s.

Kenny Hoops

181. **Otto Hoops,** US Army, served during WWII, native of Ferney.

182. **James Hostetter,** US Army/US Navy, Seaman, discharged from Army in May 1952 and enlisted in US Navy. Son of Mr. and Mrs. Enos Hostetter of Amherst. In February 1953, Hostetter was assigned to USS *Wasp* as a seaman.

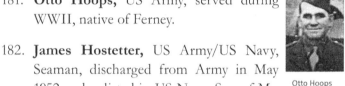
Otto Hoops

183. **Leland Houdek,** US Army, WWII veteran, served in Germany. Married to LaVerna Houdek of Groton.

184. **Harlow H. Howe,** US Navy, in March 1953, completed recruit training at the Naval Training Center, Great Lakes, Illinois. Assigned to a heavy cruiser, USS *Helena*. Son of Mr. and Mrs. C.R. Howe of Houghton.

185. **Leon E. Howe,** US Navy, Chief Machinist's Mate, in October 1963, embarked aboard the attack cargo ship USS *Merrick* which operated out of Long

Beach, California. Son of Mr. and Mrs. C.R. Howe of Houghton.

186. **Ronald Hubbard,** WWII veteran, past commander of Groton American Legion. Farm manager in Groton area.

187. **Joseph E. Hueitl,** US Army, Private in 1951. Son of Mr. and Mrs. Joe Hueitl of Columbia. Returned to Fort Hood, Texas, after a 14-day leave in Columbia. In April 1951, Hueitl attended medical field service school at Brooke Army Medical Center, San Antonio, Texas.

188. **Orville Huffman**, US Army, Mountain Arsenal Company, served from 1950 through 1953.

189. **John Huser,** US Air Force, native of Columbia, enlisted in November 1954.

190. **Lyle Dean Ives,** US Air Force, veteran of WWII served in the European Theater. Flew on 72 missions over France, Rome-Arno, and Yugoslavia. Received the Air Medal, two Silver Oak Leaf Clusters, two Bronze Oak Leaf Clusters and the Distinguished Unit Badge. Formerly of Andover and Groton areas.

191. **Thurlo H. Jark,** US Navy, native of Stratford, in March 1951, was in training at the Navy's Great Lakes, Illinois base.

192. **Kenneth Jark,** US Army, Corporal, served from 1953 through 1955, native of Stratford.

193. **Milton H. Jensen,** US Army, served in North Africa, Sicily, and Northern Italy in the Quarter Master Corps and received

Kenneth Jark

his honorable discharge in 1945. In 1962, Jensen returned to South Dakota from the West Coast and was a resident of Stratford.

194. **Wilmer Jensen,** US Army, in March 1954, furloughed with his parents, Mr. and Mrs. Oscar Jensen of Andover.

195. **Boyd Johnson,** US Army, Corporal, served from 1942 through 1946 Pacific Theater Operations, native of Columbia.

196. **Clare Johnson,** US Army/Air Force, Staff Sergeant, served from 1942 through 1945, native of Columbia.

Clare Johnson

197. **Dale Johnson,** in April 1953 returned from Korea after serving 18 months and was discharged. Son of Mr. and Mrs. Effie Johnson of Andover.

198. **Dale G. Johnson,** US Army, Private, completed basic training in Fort Riley, Kansas, February 1952. Graduate of Columbia High School.

199. **Darrel P. Johnson,** US Air Force, Airman First Class, in June 1954, received a meritorious service commendation for serving as radio operator of an unarmed transport plane while serving in support of combat units in Korea during the period of November 1952 to July 1953. Johnson enlisted in September 1950 and served in Korea for two years. Son of Mr. and Mrs. Clarence Johnson of Groton.

200. **Joseph Johnson,** US Navy, WT 2/C, served from 1943 through 1946, was awarded Asia Pacific Theater Battle Stars and Navy Citation. Native of Columbia.

201. **Joyce Johnson,** US Army, enlisted in 1945 and discharged in 1947. Worked for a few Groton area farmers after being discharged.

202. **Ralph D. Johnson,** US Navy, Engineer Second Class, in June 1952, served aboard the landing ship Rocket No. 403. In April 1954, Johnson was on leave from duty in Korea for the previous nine months. Son of Mr. and Mrs. Ralph G. Johnson of Columbia.

Ralph Johnson

203. **Walter M. Johnson,** Private, in September 1953, completed basic training and eight weeks of medical training at the Medical Replacement Training Center at Camp Pickett, Virginia. Son of Mr. and Mrs. Floyd L. Johnson of Groton.

204. **William Donald Johnson,** US Army, WWII veteran, and member of the American Legion Post #39 of Groton. Lived in Groton during his retirement years.

205. **Richard Jones**, US Army, served from 1952 through 1954.

206. **Carl Oscar Jones,** US Army, WWII. Son of Mr. and Mrs. Ralph Jones.

207. **Raymond H. Jones,** US Army Air Corps, served from 1941 to 1946 and retired after 30 years in the Air Force Reserve. Jones was born in Houghton and graduated from Hecla High School in 1933.

208. **Richard Jones,** US Army, served from 1952 to 1954. Lived in Groton and raised three children. Jones worked as a machinist at Hub City Inc.

209. **James N. Julson,** US Army, Korean War veteran. Graduated from Groton High School in 1944.

210. **Eugene E. Kammerer,** US Army, Germany, served as an interpreter 1953-1955. Graduate of Hosmer High School in 1953 and served as Principal of Groton High School until retirement. Died in 2020.

211. **Larry Karlen,** US Marine Corps, Captain, pilot, served five years in Hawaii. A 1954 graduate of Columbia High School.

212. **Paul D. Kauffman,** WWII veteran. Moved to the Groton area in 1944. Custodian at the Groton Elementary School until his retirement in 1978.

213. **Mercedes Kelly (Julson),** US Navy, SP3, WWII. Married Les Julson of Andover and taught school in the Andover and Groton school districts for over 42 years. Married John Volk from Aberdeen in 1979 and passed away at the age of 86 in 2009.

214. **Kenneth V. Karnopp**, US Navy from 1940 through 1960. Served on the aircraft carrier USS *Wasp*, fought in Guadalcanal campaign and in a battle off the Solomon

Kenneth Karnopp

Islands, during which the ship was torpedoed and sunk. He then became a plank operator on the new carrier USS *Kearsarge* during the Okinawa Campaign and the occupation of Japan. He went on to serve on the USS *Antietam*, USS *Coral Sea*, USS *Norton Sound*, USS *Suisan*, USS *Koener*, and after 20 years of service, his retirement ceremony took place on the USS *Forster* at Pearl Harbor on April 2, 1960.

215. **Ralph Karnopp**, US Army, Medical Tech, served in China, Burma, and India theatres.

216. **Wallace Karnopp,** US Navy, Seaman First Class, was lost at sea in 1944. Graduated from Groton High School in 1943.

   Wallace Karnopp

217. **Earl L. Kent,** US Army, Staff Sergeant, in September 1959, was assigned to Headquarters Company, US Army Ryukyu Islands. Kent entered the Army in 1948 and was a television equipment repairman for the company. August 1964 reenlisted in the Army for an additional six years while stationed with the Armed Forces Radio and Television Service in Okinawa. Graduate of Aberdeen Central High School and brother of Omer Nelson, Groton.

218. **Duane Kindski,** US Navy, WWII, graduate of Columbia High School.

219. **Francis Klein**, US Army, Alaska, served from 1950 through 1952.

220. **Richard (Dick) Kluge**, US Navy, served from 1954 through 1957.

221. **Donald Knapp,** US Marines, PFC, enlisted in 1941, and in 1942, Knapp went overseas and saw action on Guadalcanal, Bougainville, and the Philippines. He was killed in action in the Philippines on June 14, 1945. He was the son of Mr. and Mrs. Carl Knapp of Groton. He was born and raised in Newark, South Dakota, until his enlistment.

222. **Lois Carson Knecht,** US Army Nurse Corps, 1st Lieutenant, native of Houghton. Served from 1942 through 1945.

223. **Richard E. Knoll,** US Navy, enlisted September 1943. Served in the Pacific Theater as a deep-sea diver. He was discharged in 1945. Graduated from Groton High School in 1942.

224. **Jerrold Koehler,** US Army, served during the Korean War. Graduated from Groton High School in 1949.

225. **Thomas E. Koenig,** US Navy, Seaman Apprentice, in June 1952 served, aboard battleship USS *Wisconsin*. Son of Mr. and Mrs. Alfred Koenig of Turton.

226. **Lyle J. Koffler,** US Army, Infantry. Koffler was stationed with occupation forces in Korea.

227. **Gus Kolb,** WWII from 1943 to 1946, and Korea 1951, graduate of Leola High School, former Columbia resident, and Columbia High School superintendent and teacher. Coached

Gus Kolb

Columbia American Legion baseball in 1962. Long career of playing sports, coaching, and teaching in South Dakota. Inducted into South Dakota Sports Hall of Fame in 2018/2019. Inducted into South Dakota Basketball Coaches Hall of Fame in 2020. Died in Texas in 2018 at the age of 93.

228. **Julius Kolb**, US Army, Asiatic Pacific, from 1945 through 1946. Awarded Asiatic Pacific Service Medal, Victory Medal, and Army of Occupation Medal.

Julius Kolb

229. **Alvin Kolb,** US Army, Private, in June 1954, completed basic infantry training at Fort Leonard Wood, Missouri, with a unit of the 6th Armored Division. Husband of Beverly Kolb of Verdon.

230. **Hiram Kolbo,** US Army, 20th Armored Division. Enlisted as soon as he reached the age of 18 after graduating from Langford High School. For two years, beginning in 1943, the 20th Armored Division served stateside as a replacement training division. In February 1945, the division was deployed to Europe where it participated in the final drive in the defeat of Germany. While some units of the Division engaged in combat as it advanced to Munich and Salzburg, most units, including Hiram's, remained combat-free during their time overseas. Because of its low casualty count, the division was called the "luckiest division that departed from American shores for combat." Total wartime casualties numbered 186, with 46 killed in action. Of the 134 wounded, one was missing in action and five were prisoners of war. As the war came to an

end, Hiram toured Hitler's bunker, mountain retreat, and personal railroad car. The members of the 20th Armored Division departed from Le Havre for New York City six months to the day of their arrival. Hiram was a gunner on a half-track truck. Occupants of the half-track dubbed the vehicle as "Purple Heart Boxes."

231. **Juel Kolbo,** US Army, joined in early 1942 during his senior year at Langford High School. Finished his high school education in clerical school in the Army. Went through jungle training and was involved in several pacific island battles. As a member of the 7th Infantry Division, he was part of the landing at Okinawa on April 1, 1945, spent two and half months in that siege, and in June 1945, one day before his 21st birthday and 10 days before the end of the siege, Kolbo was blown up by a grenade at the entrance to a cave while his unit was evacuating Japanese women where they were being used as shields for Japanese soldiers. He lost his left eye, most of his teeth and suffered many other wounds. It took almost a full year to recover from those wounds. He received the Purple Heart and other service medals for his service. He saw 125 days of action at Leyte but said, "Nothing could have ever been tougher than that battle in Okinawa. We lost so many men, and so many were injured."

232. **Art Krage,** US Army, after completing basic training was assigned to Seventh US Army. Was not involved in some of the first battles of WWII, including an operation called Operation Torch in North Africa, but he joined them when the Seventh US Army invaded Southern Sicily and captured the city of Palermo. In

August 1944, Seventh US Army units assualted the beaches of southern France in the St. Ropez and St. Raphael area. While in combat there, Art was shot in his right arm and right leg. He returned to the US and recovered from his wounds at Walter Reed Hospital. He received a Purple Heart, and Bronze Star for his dedication to his country.

233. **Emil Krage,** US Army, Private First Class, served from 1944 through 1945, in the infantry and assigned to the Fifth Army. The Fifth Army was part of the Allied Forces that had successfully forced the German Army out of North Africa. It was also part of the Northern Allied forces that landed at Salerno, Italy. After four major offensives between January and May 1944 the Fifth Army and Allies advanced beyond Rome, taking Florence. It was during a battle on June 22, 1944, when Emil was shot in his left arm, shoulder and his right hand by a machine gun. He remained in a hospital in Naples for six month and another seven months in the Billings Hospital in Indiana. Emil was awarded Purple Heart, Bronze Star and European Theater of Operations medal. Native of Columbia.

234. **Jermitt Krage,** US Army. In June 1953 left by train for Fort Sheridan and was scheduled to attend Medical Technician training at Brooke Army Hospital in October. Spent time at Fort Sheridan playing baseball for ten weeks. Krage was the best available catcher. Then was assigned to Camp Pickett, VA for basic training. Because of the delay (playing baseball) from

Fort Sheridan to Camp Pickett, Krage was treated as absent without leave. Everything was worked out with the commanding officer and because he was a SD boy (commanding officer's words), all he had to do was pass the requirements on all of the shooting ranges, go through the gas chamber, throw some grenades, crawl on his belly at night while machine guns fired over his head and complete a three-day forced field march. Upon completion, he joined his basic training company and went through graduation. He spent a grand total of four weeks in basic training. He then left for Brooke Army Hospital. Mrs. Krage and daughter lived at their parent's home in Columbia during this time. A 1952 graduate of Columbia High School.

235. **John Kranzler,** WWII veteran, served in Algeria French-Morocco Campaign, Tunisia Campaign, Sicilian Campaign, and at Normandy. In early 1970s, Kranzler moved to Groton.

236. **Arlan L. Krege,** US Army, Private, in May 1956, graduated from supply handling course at Quarter Master School, Fort Lee, Virginia. Krege entered Army in December 1955 and completed basic training at Fort Chafee, Alaska. In June 1956, Krege was assigned to Alaska at the Port of Whittier. Graduate of Columbia High School. Son of Henry W. Krege of Columbia.

237. **Walter Kroll**, US Army, Sergeant, served from 1953 through 1955. In April 1954, left duty in Fort Lewis, Washington, for duty in the Pacific. Son of Mr. and Mrs. Gunther Kroll of Andover.

238. **Leon F. Krueger,** US Army, Private, in 1951. Son of Mr. and Mrs. Fred Krueger of Verdon. Assigned to the Medical Replacement Training Center, a unit of Brooke Army Medical Center, San Antonio, Texas.

239. **Peter Kryger (Doctor),** veteran of Dutch Army and was in the underground during WWII. Practiced medicine in Groton.

240. **Harley J. Kruse,** US Navy, Seaman Recruit, in February 1956 Kruse spent 17-day furlough in Columbia. At the end of the furlough, reported to Oak Harbor, Washington, for assignment. Native of Columbia.

241. **Dean Kurtz,** veteran of WWII. Lived in Groton area his entire life.

242. **Lynn C. LaBrie,** US Navy, Sonarman Third Class, in June 1956, selected to assist the company commanders after training at the Naval Training Center, Great Lakes, Illinois. In August 1956, LaBrie reported to Key West, Florida. In September 1959 he served aboard the destroyer USS *Cone* operating as part of the 6th Fleet in the Mediterranean. Son of Mr. and Mrs. Leon C. LaBrie of Turton.

243. **Arthur Lange**, US Navy, Signalman 2nd Class, served on SS *Cape Newenhorn* in Pacific Theater, from 1943 through 1945.

Art Lange

244. **Charles Lapham,** US Air Force, Staff Sergeant, furloughed in July 1956 to visit parents, Mr. and Mrs. H.W. Lapham of

Andover. Lapham had been assigned to an air force base in England for four years. Married an English girl while there. He was then sent to Fairchild Air Force Base near Spokane, Washington, for further duty. At the completion of his 18-month assignment in WA, Lapham would have served eight years in the Air Force. In March 1959, he spent a 30-day furlough with his parents, wife, and daughter in Andover. Left for assignment in Germany at the expiration of the furlough.

245. **Gordon E. Lapham,** US Navy, WWII veteran. Lapham was born in Andover.

246. **Robert H. Lapham,** US Navy, WWII veteran. Graduated from Andover High School in 1943.

247. **Francis J. Larson,** US Army, reported for physical in October 1951. He was assigned to Camp Breckenridge, Kentucky, in January 1952. Graduated from Columbia High School in 1948.

248. **Merle F. Larson,** US Army, Private, in February 1954, completed eight weeks of training at Fort Riley, Kansas. Assigned to Fort Belvoir, Virginia, and enrolled in an engineering school. Son of Mr. and Mrs. Lloyd Larson of Columbia.

249. **Arlo Layton,** US Army, Private First Class, in March 1955, served with 62nd Transport Truck Co, Karlsruhe, Germany. Layton is the nephew of Mr. and Mrs. Herman Krage of Columbia.

250. **Delbert Leonhardt,** US Army, served in France and Germany from 1953 through 1955.

Delbert Leonhardt

251. **Leon D. Lemmon,** US Air Force, Airman First Class, in June 1954 assigned as Senior Clerk at 5th Air Force Headquarters in Korea. Lemmon had been in the Air Force since January 1952. Son of Mr. and Mrs. William Lemmon and husband of Shirley Lemmon of Andover.

252. **Ward Lemmon,** US Navy, Coxswain, enlisted in 1941 and discharged in 1943. Graduated from Andover High School in 1941.

Ward Lemmon

253. **Glenn A. Lenling,** US Air Force, in April 1953, completed basic training at Lackland Air Force Base, Texas. Son of Mr. and Mrs. Waldemar Lenling of Groton. 1950 graduate of Groton High School.

254. **Edward Lilla/Norbert Lilla,** US Army, served in Africa, Sicily, and Italy where Edward met his brother Norbert. Two of Edward's sons served in Vietnam and two in the South Dakota Army National Guard. One grandson took part in Operation Iraqi Freedom. Both Edward and Norbert were from Hecla.

255. **Raymond Lilly,** US Army, Sergeant, killed in action in 1944, in England. Served 1943–1944, European Theater of Operations. Native of Andover.

Raymond Lilly

256. **Herman Lier,** US Air Force, Airman First Class, served from 1950 through 1954 in Okinawa, Japan. Awarded Korean Service, U.N. Service, and National Defense Service Medal. Native of Putney.

257. **Donald M. Lindert,** US Navy, enlisted when he was 17. Attended Groton High School.

Herman Lier

258. **Clayton Litch,** US Army, Corporal, served from 1947 through 1953. Stationed in Korea during the Korean War. Attained the rank of corporal in the 2nd Infantry Division. Was awarded the Korean Service Medal three times. Worked for the Groton Truck Center in Groton, and in 1985, Litch moved to Pierpont.

259. **Ervin Locke,** US Army, drafted in 1954 and had to leave a promising college career as a standout football player. Served most of his time in service in Company B., 12th Engineer Battalion at Fort Carson, Colorado. Served as police officer in Groton, owned and operated the Red Horse until his death and was mayor of Groton from 1984 to 1990.

Ervin Locke

260. **Darwin R. Lovell,** US Army, in February 1951 awarded Combat Infantry Badge with 7th Cavalry Regiment, Korea. Assigned to the front lines in February 1951, Lovell was wounded on February 14, 1951, and subsequently hospitalized in Japan. Son of Mr. and Mrs. Chester Lovell of Andover.

261. **William G. Lovell,** US Army, Sergeant, discharged in December 1951 after four years in Army. Served three and a half years in Germany. Son of Mr. and Mrs. Chester Lovell of Andover.

262. **Eugene Luce**, US Marines, Corporal, served in the Pacific Theater, from 1942 through 1945.

263. **John F. Luce,** US Army, served from 1951 to 1953. Formerly a resident of Groton prior to his death.

Eugene Luce

264. **Donald Lyons,** US Air Force, in December 1955, was stationed at Ellsworth Air Force Base, Rapid City, South Dakota. Scheduled for duty in January 1956. Lyons and family arrived in Andover to visit relatives.

265. **Eugene M. Lyons,** US Marines, Private First Class, arrived in Korea in October 1952 with First Marine Division. In July 1953, Lyons returned from spending a year in Korea to Andover for a 30-day furlough and returned to Camp Pendleton, California, for discharge. Son of Mr. and Mrs. Royal Lyons of Andover.

266. **Stanley Markley,** US Air Force, entered the Air Force after he graduated from Groton High School in 1950.

267. **Richard Marske**, US Army, served from 1953 through 1955. In May 1955, Marske was stationed in training camp in Georgia. Furloughed to visit parents, Mr. and Mrs. E.O. Marske of Andover.

268. **Bertell Martin,** US Army National Guard, served several years. Born in Groton.

269. **Donald E. Martin,** US Army, Private, entered Army in October 1953 and was stationed at Fort Riley, Kansas, as of December 1953. Son of Mr. and Mrs. Edward Martin of Andover.

270. **Robert Martin,** US Navy, veteran of WWII, graduate of Columbia High School.

271. **Robert Matheny,** US Army, served from 1942 through 1946 with the 12th Armored Division, European Theater of Operation.

272. **Alan K. McFarlane,** South Dakota State Guard during WWII, 1943 graduate of Groton High School.

Alan McFarlane

James McKane

273. **James McKane Jr.,** US Army Air Corps, Staff Sergeant, served from 1940 through 1945 in Asia Pacific Theater of Operations, awarded Asia Pacific Theater, American Defense/Bronze Star, and Air Medal/Oak Leaf Cluster. Native of Andover.

Dale McGannon

274. **Dale McGannon**, US Air Force, served from 1951 through 1955, in Germany, Colorado, and New Mexico.

275. **Jim McKittrick,** US Army, enlisted in 1953 and was discharged in 1955. He served in Fort Leonard Wood, Missouri, and Fort Lewis, Washington. Resident of Groton at the time of his death. Graduated from Bristol High School.

Jim McKittrick

276. **LaVerl "Mac" McLaughlin,** US Army, enlisted in 1955 in Fort Meade, Maryland. Graduate of Britton High School. Resident of Groton when he passed away.

277. **Donald Erwin Meister,** US Marines, served from December 1954 until 1957. Attended school in Groton.

278. **Gerald Meister,** US Army, retired as an officer. Born in Groton.

279. **Lou Merkel,** US Army, discharged in 1946. In 1967, Merkel moved to Groton where he worked on area farms until his retirement.

280. **Floyd W. Mertz,** US Army Air Corps, discharged from the service in 1946. Born near Houghton. Moved to Hecla in 1996.

281. **Robert Mertz,** US Army, graduated from Columbia High School in 1954.

282. **Anton Meyer,** US Army, Master Sergeant, served from 1937 to 1959, stationed in Asia Pacific Theater and Korea, awarded Asia Pacific Theater/2 Clusters, Distinguished Unit/Oak Leaf Cluster, and Presidential Unit Citation. Native of Andover.

Anton Meyer

283. **Leo Meyer,** US Army, Corporal, in December 1956, arrived home after receiving his discharge from the Army. Previously served 18 months in Hawaii. Resident of Andover.

284. **Clarence Mielke,** US Navy Seabee, WWII ended while on the ship headed for combat.

285. **Donald Miller,** US Army, enlisted after graduating from Gettysburg High School near the end of WWII. Miller lived in Groton from 1997 until his death in 2006.

286. **Maurice Miller,** US Army, graduated from Columbia High School in 1948.

287. **William F. Miller,** veteran of WWII. Member of the Conde American Legion and the Redfield VFW.

288. **Arthur E. Mills,** US Army, Major, Chaplain, in April 1956, was appointed post chaplain at Fort Monroe, Virginia. Enlisted in Army in December 1943 and except for a break in service between 1946 and 1948, Mills served continuously until retirement. He served with the 81st Infantry Division in the Pacific during WWII and with the 1st Cavalry Division during the Korean War. Former resident of Andover.

289. **Vernon Misslitz,** US Navy, Seaman Second Class, served from 1943 through 1946, native of Stratford.

290. **John C. Mohn,** US Marines, Corporal, in December 1954, spent a 30-day furlough with his parents Mr. and Mrs. J.C. Mohn of Andover. Mohn was stationed at Camp Lejeune, North Carolina. In July 1956, Mohn arrived home after being discharged from the Marines.

291. **Robert Molgard,** US Army Air Corps, served from 1946 to October 1947. Prior to his death, Molgard was the administrator of the Colonial Manor at Groton.

292. **Diana Morehouse,** US Marines, Corporal in 1952. Daughter of Mr. and Mrs. Archie Morehouse of Andover.

Assigned to Marine Barracks, Camp Lejeune, North Carolina, to begin 13 weeks in a marine supply school. In September 1952, she was discharged after serving in Supply Depot at San Francisco, California. Visited Andover before moving to Indianapolis, Indiana, to join her husband.

293. **Donald L. Morehouse,** US Army, Specialist 3rd Class, in October 1956, promoted to specialist 3rd class in Korea where he was a gunner in Battery A of the 7th Infantry Division. Entered the Army in January 1955 and completed basic training at Fort Knox, Kentucky. Received his discharge from the Army at Fort Lewis, Washington. He had served 16 months in Korea before receiving his discharge. Graduate of Bristol High School and son of Mr. and Mrs. Lloyd Morehouse of Andover.

294. **Ivan Morehouse,** US Army, served from 1952 through 1954, native of Andover. Graduated from Andover High School in 1940.

295. **Robert Murray,** US Army, served as a teletype operator in Saipan from December 1944 to September 1946. Graduated from Groton High School in 1942.

296. **Homer Mydland**, US Navy, Purple Heart recipient, Aleutian Islands, served from 1943 through 1946.

Homer Mydland

297. **Darrell Nack,** US Air Force, served from 1951 through 1954, discharged with a rank of staff sergeant. 1949 Groton High School graduate.

Darrell Nack

298. **Elmer Nash**, US Army, served from 1953 through 1955.

Elmer Nash

Frank Nehls

299. **Frank Nehls,** no information available.

300. **Lyle Nehls,** member of the Groton American Legion.

301. **Ralph Nehls**, US Navy, served two years during WWII.

Lyle Nehls

302. **Richard Nehls**, US Army, served in 1944. Attended school in Ferney. Moved to Groton in 1951.

303. **Grant Nelson,** graduate of Columbia High School.

304. **Duane Neuman,** stationed in Japan after WWII. A 1946 graduate of Groton High School.

Duane Neuman

305. **Chuck "Duke" Nietert,** US Navy, WWII veteran. Graduated from Claremont High School in 1942.

306. **Jack Nissen,** US Army, Corporal in 1952. Son of Mr. and Mrs. Hans Nissen of Groton. After training in Fort Riley, Kansas, he was assigned to Fort Lawton, Washington. Returned from the Far East in April 1952. 1947 graduate of Groton High School.

307. **Herman Nilsson,** served in WWII from 1942 through 1945. Wounded while serving on the Japanese island of Okinawa and was honorably discharged. Moved to Groton in 1964, where he lived until his death.

308. **Robert E. Nogle,** US Navy, Chief Carpenter's Mate in the 63rd Naval Construction Battalion from 1942 through 1945. Graduated from Groton High School.

309. **Gary D. Odland,** US Navy, enlisted in December 1953. In July 1954, Odland was assigned to USS *Haynesworth* at Norfolk, Virginia. Graduated from Claremont High School in 1952. Son of Mr. and Mrs. Elmer Odland of Houghton.

Gary Odland

310. **Robert A. Olson Sr.,** US Navy, Seaman Recruit, in December 1955, spent leave with parents Mr. and Mrs. Arthur Olson of Andover. In February 1956, Olson Sr. completed boot training at Great Lakes Naval Training Center, assigned to radioman school at Norfolk, Virginia. In December 1957, after a 30-day leave with his family in Andover, he returned to duty at a naval station near San Diego, California. Husband of the former Audrey Easterby of Andover.

311. **Robert J. Olson,** US Navy, served from 1950 through 1954, teletype operator on several battleships in Korean waters during Korean War. 33½ years as an educator including superintendent of Groton Public School system. Retired in Groton and passed away in 2006 at the age of 76.

Robert Olson

312. **Eddy Opp**, US Army, served from 1953 through 1955.

Eddy Opp

313. **James B. Osness,** US Army, Private First Class in 1951. Son of Mr. and Mrs. Melvin Osness of Andover. Entered the Airplane and Engine Mechanic's School at Sheppard Air Force Base, Wichita Falls, Texas.

314. **Robert L. Osness,** US Air Force, enlisted in July 1951, native of Andover.

315. **Arthur Padfield,** US Army, enlisted in 1942, and was an airplane mechanic. Discharged in 1945. Attended school in Verdon. Employed by Jay Swisher and Clark Brothers Farm for 32 years. Later worked for Pioneer Ford and Olive Grove Golf course until he retired at the age of 90.

316. **Gerald Paetznick,** US Air Force, enlisted in November 1951, native of Groton.

317. **Helmuth Paetznick,** US Navy, in December 1957, received his separation papers from the Navy after four years of service. A 1953 graduate of Groton High School. Son of Mrs. Henry Paetznick of Groton.

318. **Reuban Paul,** US Army, Pacific Theater. Bronze star and Purple Heart. Survived by Diane Gibbs (Paul) of Groton.

Reuban Paul

319. **Stanley J. Pavek,** US Navy, served from 1942 through 1945, and graduated from Claremont High School in 1939.

320. **DeWain Peterson,** US Army, enlisted in 1941. Part of the 17th Regiment and was stationed in the Aleutian Islands. Then stationed in Honolulu, Hawaii,

DeWain Peterson

where DeWain took part in the joint operations between the Navy and Army against the Japanese-held Kwajalein Island. He was injured in both the shoulder and wrist by artillery fire on the Philippine Islands.

321. **Howard H. Peterson**, US Army, Korean War, and WWII.

322. **Ralph Peterson,** US Army, served from 1942 through 1945.

Ralph Peterson

323. **Alfred "Ed" Phillips Jr.,** US Army, stationed in Germany. In 1978, he moved to the Groton area where he started his salvage yard business.

324. **Duane R. Pierson,** US Army, WWII veteran. Graduated from Claremont High School in 1942. Upon discharged, Pierson returned to Houghton/Groton area.

325. **Wesley Pierson**, US Navy, served from 1942 through 1946. Graduated from Claremont High School.

326. **Allan Pigors,** US Army, enlisted in December 1953, native of Andover.

327. **Donald A. Pigors,** US Army, Sergeant, served from 1952 through 1955, veteran of Korean War, and awarded Korean War Service, U.N. Service, and National Defense medals. Native of Andover.

328. **Herbert Pigors,** US Army Air Corps, served in the Pacific Theater at New Guinea. Born and raised in the Ferney/Groton area.

329. **Ray Pitschka**, US Navy, served from 1942 through 1944.

330. **Emerson R. Place,** US Navy, Dispersing Clerk 3rd Class, reported on board escort vessel, USS *Alvin C. Cockrell*, March 1955. Son of Mrs. Hopner of Stratford.

Robert Podoll

Vernon Podoll

331. **Robert Podoll,** US Army, 88th Infantry in European Theater. Killed in action in Salerno, Italy in October 1944. Brothers, **Erling** and **Vernon,** served in the Pacific Theater. All born and raised in Westport/ Columbia area.

Norman Pray

332. **Norman A. Pray,** US Army Air Corps, stationed at Weaver Air Base (now Ellsworth) part of the time. Served from 1943 to 1946. Graduated from Groton High School in 1935.

333. **Robert Pray Sr.,** US Navy, S1C AMM CAC, served from 1944 through 1946, was awarded American Area and WWII Victory medals. A 1942 graduate of Groton High School.

Robert Pray

334. **Clarence Prunty,** Lieutenant, in July 1954, was on furlough with his parents, Mr. and Mrs. Francis P. Prunty of Andover, prior to going to Seattle, Washington, for further assignment.

335. **William N. Prunty,** US Army, Private First Class, in June 1954, underwent basic infantry training at Fort Leonard Wood, Missouri. In December 1954, Prunty graduated from radio operator's course at Camp Gordon, Georgia. In January 1955, he was assigned to 511th Airborne Signal Co of the 11th Airborne Division as a clerk typist in company headquarters. In March 1955, he completed 11th Airborne Division airborne school. Son of Francis P. Prunty of Andover.

336. **Scott Pulfrey,** US Army, in 1945, served in the European Theater of Operations, native of Columbia.

337. **Ted Pulfrey,** US Army, served in 1945 in the South Pacific Theater of Operations, native of Columbia.

338. **Wayne Quiggle Sr.,** US Army, served from 1940 through 1942. Returned to farm near Groton.

339. **Bert Raap**, US Army, from 1953 through 1955. In January 1955, returned home to Andover after receiving his discharge from the Army. Raap joined his wife, Darlene Sturm, and daughter at the home of Henry Sturm.

340. **Verril Radke,** US Navy, Coxswain, served from 1944 through 1946, native of Stratford.

341. **Leonard L. Ragels,** US Air Force, in June 1952, graduated from Air Defense Artillery school at Memphis, Tennessee. Assigned to a patrol squadron at San Diego, California. Son of Mr. and Mrs. Chester Ragels of Groton.

Verril Radke

342. **Donley W. Raines**, US Navy Seabees, Yeoman 1C, Hawaii, served from 1943 through 1946. "My father never talked about his service. He did tell me that he typically sent home more money to his parents than he earned, thanks to his poker playing ability." Awarded American Campaign, Asia Pacific Theater Ribbon, and Victory Medals. He graduated from Flandreau High School in 1942 and the University of South Dakota in 1950. Father of Lee T. Raines and Susan Raines Jahraus who graduated from Groton High School in 1971 and 1972, respectively.

Donley Raines

343. **Darrel R. Ramford,** US Air Force, entered service in December 1951, completed aircraft mechanical school and began B-36 mechanic specialist course. Native of Turton.

344. **Charles Rehfuss,** US Army, entered military service in 1943 and stationed at Camp Wolters Army Training Base in Texas until he was sent to England in 1944. He served in the European Theater of Operations until his discharge in 1946. Graduated from Groton High School in 1929.

345. **James Richardson,** US Army, graduated from Columbia High School in 1951.

346. **David LaVerne Richardson,** US Marines, graduated from Columbia High School.

347. **Donald J. Ries,** US Army, served in the European/African/Middle Eastern Theaters in Northern France,

Rhineland, and Central Europe. After he was discharged, moved to Groton.

348. **Jean P. Ries,** US Army, assigned to Australia and New Guinea during WWII. First group of Americans to set foot in Australia during WWII. Left Hawaii seven days before Pearl Harbor was attacked.

349. **Merrill Rix,** US Army Air Corps, WWII, mechanic, stationed in Guam and Saipan from 1944 through 1945. Graduated from Groton High School in 1932.

Merrill Rix

350. **Mathieu Rock,** US Army, enlisted in 1942, WWII veteran. Served with the 1255th H&S Company until his discharge in 1946. Graduated from Groton High School in 1942.

351. **Arlo Roettele,** US Army, graduated from Columbia High School in 1952.

352. **Myron Rose,** US Air Force.

353. **Joe Rossman,** US Navy, in April 1951, assigned to communications technical school in San Diego, California. Son of Mr. and Mrs. Joe Rossman of Columbia.

Myron Rose

354. **Dallas Rossow,** US Air Force, enlisted December 1951 and served until December 1956. Graduated from Groton High School in 1951.

355. **Gordon M. Rossow,** US Army, Private, in October 1954, began his eight-week basic training at the Anti-Aircraft Artillery Replacement Training Center, Fort Bliss, Texas. A 1953 graduate of Groton High School. Son of Mr. and Mrs. Marvin E. Rossow of Stratford.

356. **Joe Rossman,** US Army, veteran of WWII, graduated in 1948 from Columbia High School.

357. **Beven Roth,** US Army, veteran of WWII, discharged in 1946, First Cavalry Division Band, graduate of Columbia High School.

358. **George C. Rowbotham,** US Army Air Corps, served from 1947 through 1949. Moved to Groton in 1981.

359. **Clara (Ruden) Rix,** 1st Lieutenant, Women's Army Corps. Nurse in field surgical hospitals. Member of the 12th General Hospital Unit. Stationed in Algeria, Naples, Casablanca, and then sent back to New York City. Returned to Aberdeen as a private duty nurse.

Clara Ruden Rix

360. **Richard Sampson,** US Navy, served from 1952 through 1956 during Korean War. Graduate of Pierpont High School.

361. **Harold E. Samuel**, US Army, enlisted on January 11, 1945, and was discharged on December 29, 1946. Assigned to the Philippines and Okinawa, Japan. Graduated from Groton High School in 1944. Returned to Groton and married Velma Radke and worked for Jack's Bottle Gas and the City of Groton. Passed away in 1975.

362. **Delbert "Red" Sanderson,** US Army, served from 1944 through 1946, in Okinawa, Japan and Korea. Former resident of Groton. Confirmed and married in Groton. Born in Verdon.

363. **Howard Sanderson,** US Army, returned home to Houghton after serving 16 months in Korea. Served in the Army postal department during his Korean assignment. Inducted in April 1951, and he is the son of Mr. and Mrs. Allen Sanderson of Houghton.

364. **Laverne G. Saunders**, Brigadier General, US Air Force, born in Stratford in 1903. Graduated from the University of South Dakota in 1924 and the US Military Academy in 1928. In 1941, Saunders was a major, commanding the 12th Bombardment Group, at Hickam Field, Hawaii. One of the few to get a bomber into the air after the Japanese surprise attack but too late to find or strike the Japanese fleet. Beginning in 1942, Saunders' B-17 group was operating south of Guadalcanal, and other occupied islands in the Solomons, attacking Japanese shipping, aircraft, and shore installations. Air advisor to Admiral William F. Halsey during the Solomons operations. Commanding general of the VII Bomber Command and Chief of Staff of the Seventh Air Force. Led group in destroying 60 enemy planes, damaging 33 others, and crippling an aircraft carrier and other vessels. Became a Deputy Chief of Air Staff stationed in Washington DC in 1943. Earned the Navy's highest decoration—the Navy Cross—as well as the Distinguished Service Medal, Distinguished

Laverne Saunders

Flying Cross, Silver Star, and Purple Heart with cluster. In 1943, he was assigned the task of overall organization and training of the first B-29 air wing—the 58th Bomb Wing (Very Heavy). In 1944, 68 B-29s under General Saunders flew against the iron and steel works at Yamato, Japan. In 1944 Saunders' B-25 crashed. He spent the next two and a half years in the hospital and retired in 1947. Saunders Field Airport in Aberdeen, South Dakota, is named after him. His son Richard Saunders joined the Army in 1955, served in Vietnam and was a career officer. Retired from the Army as a colonel after 28 years of service with the Signal Corps and died in 2008.

Thomas Saunders

365. **Thomas Saunders,** US Army Air Force, Sergeant, served from 1943 through 1946, native of Stratford.

366. **Lawrence Schafer,** US Navy, Chief Machinist Mate, served on the USS *Blackwood* (destroyer escort) and USS *Decatur* (destroyer). Discharged in 1947. Graduated from Andover High School in 1940.

Benny Schaller

367. **Benny Schaller,** US Air Force, Military Police, England, served from 1951 through 1955. Sent to San Antonio, Texas, for two months of basic training and then to Camp Gordon in Georgia for two months of combat training. After 18 months of military police duty at Roswell, New Mexico, Schaller was sent to Fairford Air Force Base in England for 30 months where he

guarded the A-Bomb. A 1950 graduate of Groton High School.

368. **Kenny Schaller,** US Air Corps, served from 1944 through 1946, graduated from Groton High School in 1944.

Kenny Schaller

369. **Wally Schaller,** US Army, enlisted after high school graduation and served in the South Pacific with a truck company until his discharge in 1946. Graduated from Groton High School in 1943.

Wally Schaller

370. **Edwin Scheid**, US Navy, served from 1945 through 1946.

371. **Orville Schlichting,** US Navy, Machinist Mate Second Class, served from 1945 through 1947, Japan. Awarded Pacific Theater, Victory, and Occupation/Japan medals. Native of Stratford.

372. **Marvin Schliebe,** US Navy, Machinist's Mate, Petty Officer Second Class, from Aberdeen. Married to Goldie Bernice Meyers Schliebe of Groton. Died at sea on January 14, 1946. Survived by a wife and daughter. Schliebe is memorialized at Tablets of the Missing at Honolulu Memorial, Hawaii. Awarded World War II Victory Medal, Purple Heart, Combat Action Ribbon, American Campaign Medal, Navy Presidential Unit Citation, Navy Good Conduct Medal, Asiatic-Pacific Campaign Medal, and Navy Expeditionary Medal.

373. **Ray Dean Schliebe,** US Navy, in December 1955, was furloughed after completing basic training at Great Lakes Naval Training Station. Subsequently was to report for general sea duty. Graduate of Columbia High School.

374. **Dialo Schmidt,** US Army, Sergeant (T), served from 1952 through 1954. He was awarded Korean Service, Bronze Service Star and U.N. Service medals. Native of Columbia.

375. **Wilmar F. Schimmel,** US Army, Private First Class, in March 1956, took part in a training exercise held by the 4th Infantry Division in Germany. Schimmel was a gunner in Battery A of the division's 46th Anti-Aircraft Battalion. Entered Army in September 1954 and completed basic training at Fort Bliss, Texas. Son of Francis F. Schimmel of Andover.

376. **Duane A. Schley,** US Air Force, Lieutenant, in March 1951, attended electronics fundamentals course at Keesler Air Force Base, Mississippi. Native of Stratford.

377. **Marvin R. Schley,** US Army, reported for physical in September 1951. Finished basic training and specialized Fire Direction Center training at Fort Sill, Oklahoma. Sent to Germany and assigned to field artillery duties. Enlisted in 1951 and was discharged in 1959. Son of Mr. and Mrs. Armund T. Schley of Stratford.

378. **Lloyd Schlichting,** US Army, served as a combat infantryman in the European Theater of Operations and was wounded in action April 1945. Along with

being awarded the Purple Heart, he also earned Combat Infantry Badge, the Bronze Star, and Good Conduct Medal as well as the European Theater of Operations Ribbon, with two stars. Was discharged in 1946. After being discharged, Schlichting returned to Groton High School and graduated in 1947.

379. **George Schmidt,** US Air Force, served from 1951 to January 1954. Attended school in Groton.

380. **James D. Schmidt,** US Army, Staff Sergeant, in July 1953, was awarded the Commendation Ribbon for service with the Far East Air Forces (FEAF). The citation was for meritorious service with the courier section and the classified radio branch of FEAF from October 1950 to June 1953. Son of Mr. and Mrs. Nicholas Schmidt of Andover.

381. **James Schmidt,** US Air Force, Staff Sergeant, in June 1960, was named outstanding non-commissioned officer of the 3rd Weather Wing at Offutt Air Force Base, NB. Schmidt enlisted in December 1953 and was the son of Mr. and Mrs. Nickolas Schmidt of Andover. In January 1961, Schmidt was involved in an automobile/train accident in Japan. His son, Jack, survived, but James, his wife, daughter, another son, and his wife's parents were killed. Jack was returned to his grandparents in Andover, and he graduated from Groton High School in 1972.

382. **Peter N. Schmidt,** US Army, in August 1951 arrived in Seattle, aboard a US Navy transport from his tour of duty in Korea. Native of Andover.

383. **Richard A. Schmidt,** US Air Force, Airman Third Class, in October 1952, reported to Fairchild Air Force Base, Spokane, Washington. Son of Mr. and Mrs. Nick Schmidt of Andover.

384. **Rodney E. Schmidt,** US Marines, Private First Class, in February 1953, left for the Marine Base, San Diego, California. Son of Mr. and Mrs. Nick Schmidt of Andover.

385. **Kathy Shore,** US Navy Waves, graduated from Columbia High School in 1948.

386. **J. F. Sherman,** US Army, served 38 years, retired in 1957. Married Jessie V. Rix from Groton in September 1923.

387. **George W. Schoch,** US Navy, called back from reserves in May 1951, transferred back to Japan from Korea where he served for nine months. His wife, the former Bonnie Hagen taught in the primary school department at Groton.

388. **Robert W. Schreiber,** US Army, 147th Field Artillery Regiment from 1940 to 1945. He married Kathy Blair of Groton in 1964.

389. **Melvin Schroeder,** US Army, in May 1956, received his discharge from the Army. Had spent his enlistment in Germany and France. Son of Mrs. Hulda Schroeder of Andover.

390. **Lyle Schuelke,** US Army, enlisted in 1942. Graduated from Groton High School.

391. **Robert Schuelke**, US Army, Captain, 103rd Infantry Division, Europe, Purple Heart recipient, Combat Infantry Badge, Bronze Star, European Battle Stars (3), from 1943 through 1947. 1940 graduate of Groton High School.

Robert Schuelke

392. **Lawrence (Smokey) Schuring,** US Army, was stationed in the Pacific during WWII. Brother of Robert Schuring of Andover. After the war, he was later stationed at the Depot in Igloo, South Dakota, from the late 1950s until it closed in 1967. The Depot was the Black Hills Ordnance Depot. It was a munitions storage and maintenance facility formerly operated by the Ordinance Corps of the US Army. The Depot was in Fall River County, in far southwestern South Dakota about eight miles south of Edgemont. Over the years, the Depot was used for storage and testing of chemical weapons, including sarin and mustard gas. Additionally, during WWII, the site also held Italian prisoners of war. Robert Schuring's grandson Travis Schuring was on active duty with the US Air Force for 15 years after graduating from the South Dakota State University and is now an officer in the South Dakota Air National Guard in Sioux Falls, South Dakota. He served in Iraq during the Gulf War.

393. **Charles Schwab,** US Army, in January 1955, returned home to Andover after receiving his discharge from the Army. Schwab was to live with his mother, Mrs. Magdalena Schwab.

394. **Vern A. Sieber,** US Army, Master Sergeant, led 31 men through Germany in WWII with support of a halftrack with a 50-caliber machine gun mounted on it. Attended Aberdeen High School for one year, starting in 1937. He started farming after WWII until 1958 when he brought his family to Columbia. He was hired by Mr. Fritz Meintz to assist on his sheep farm. In 1962, Vern started attending the trade school in Wahpeton, North Dakota and became a licensed plumber. He was elected mayor of Columbia in the mid-1960s and remained mayor until his death in January 1974. He was a long-time member of the American Legion.

395. **George H. Siefkes,** US Army, veteran of WWII.

396. **Roland (Bill) Sieh,** US Navy, enlisted in 1941 as an Apprentice Seaman First Class, making $21 per month. Served aboard USS *Maryland* in 1942 and commissioned as an ensign; pay was $200 a month. Final rank Lieutenant. Served from 1941 through 1945. USS *Maryland* patrolled the area around Midway for 60 days about the time of the battle that took place June 4-7. He took the train home at the end of the war and arrived at the Groton depot at 6 a.m. He remained in the Naval Reserve for 10 years.

Bill Sieh

397. **John Sieh,** US Army, honorably discharged from Fort Smith, Arkansas. Attended high school in Groton.

398. **Vern Donald (Bud) Siefkes,** US Air Force, enlisted in August 1950 and was discharged September 1954. Awarded National Defense Service Medal, Korean Service Medal, and UN Service Medal. Basic/technical training at Chanute Air Force Base, Illinois, and in August 1952, Siefkes boarded USS *Anderson* for the Port of Yokohama, Japan. During the Korean War, Siefkes serviced bombers coming back from Korea. His son, Greg Siefkes, enlisted in the South Dakota National Guard, serving from 1975 through 1983. Greg graduated from Groton High School in 1975.

Bud Siefkes

399. **Donald Simonson,** US Army, enlisted February 1942 and was shipped overseas in August of that year with the 831st Engineer Aviation Battalion. Initially the unit built an airfield in Swansea, Wales. In 1944, the unit restored Orley Airfield near Paris to full use and then to Augsburg, Germany, when the war ended. Discharged in November 1945 and returned to Groton to farm. Served from 1942 through 1945. Awarded European-African-Middle Eastern Campaign Medal, WWII Army of Occupation, and Efficiency-Honor-Fidelity medals.

Donald Simonson

400. **Harry B. Simonson,** US Army, served September from 1940 through April 1944. Received New Guinea Campaign Star.

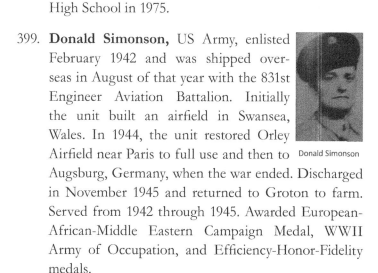

401. **Orville Simonson,** US Navy, joined the Navy in 1940 and retired from the military in 1960 as Chief Aviation Machinists Mate. Graduated from Groton High School in 1940 and immediately joined the Navy.

Orville Simonson

402. **Richard Simpson**, US Navy, Korea, served from 1952 through 1956.

403. **Blaine C. Sippel,** US Navy for three years. Spent his boyhood in the Groton and Pierpont areas and graduated from Pierpont High School in 1943.

404. **Emery Sippel**, US Navy, ABM AG 2C, Guam, Okinawa, and Philippines Islands, served from 1943 through 1946. Spent two years stationed on the *Prince William* aircraft carrier on the lookout for submarines. A 1941 graduate of Groton High School.

Emery Sippel

405. **Orylin Sippel,** served during the Korean War. Born in Groton to Mr. and Mrs. Clarence Sippel.

406. **Ralph Sippel,** US Army, served from 1950 to 1952. Graduated from Groton High School in 1944.

407. **Dialo Schmidt,** US Army, 1951 graduate of Columbia High School.

408. **Donald J. Smilloff,** US Army, in July 1953, graduated from 16 weeks of basic military training at Camp Chaffee, Alaska. Assigned to Camp Kilmer, New Jersey, to await assignment in Europe. Son of Mr. and Mrs. John Smilloff of Columbia.

409. **Herron Smith**, US Air Force, 1947. Served in Guam. Resident of Groton and formerly of Andover before his death in 2009.

410. **Curtis D. Sombke,** US Army, entered the Army in October 1954, and in December 1954, was assigned to Anti-Aircraft Training Center, Fort Bliss, Texas. In June 1955, Sombke was a member of the 753rd Anti-Aircraft Artillery Battalion in Japan. Graduated from Groton High School in 1953. Son of Mr. and Mrs. Alvin Sombke of Verdon.

Curtis Sombke

411. **Duane L. Sombke,** US Army, Private, in February 1956, parachuted into Thailand with units of 506th Airborne Regimental Combat Team. Sombke was regularly stationed in Japan. Entered Army in January 1955 and completed basic training at Fort Ord, California. Son of Mr. and Mrs. Roy Sombke of Andover.

412. **Gerald G. Sombke,** US Navy, in September 1955, returned to his ship, USS *Devel* at Norfolk, Virginia, after a 15-day leave with his parents, Mr. and Mrs. Edward Sombke of Verdon. A 1954 graduate of Groton High School.

413. **James A. Sombke,** US Air Force, Private, enlisted in November 1951. Attended basic training at Lackland Air Force Base. Son of Mr. Clarence Sombke of Verdon.

414. **Ronald C. Spear,** US Army, Specialist Third Class, in 1957 promoted while serving with the 67th AAA Battalion in Germany. Entered the Army in April 1955 and completed basic training at Fort Chaffee, Alaska,

before arriving overseas in February 1956. Son of Mr. and Mrs. A.C. Spear of Turton.

415. **Morris Spencer**, US Army, 82nd Airborne Infantry, section leader of a heavy machine gun squad. Nineteen months in European Theater including battles in Normandy, Ardennes, Rhineland, and Central Europe. Awarded four Campaign Stars and Bronze Arrowhead. Bronze Star Medal for action in Holland and received the Distinguished Unit Badge Belgian Fourragere and Order of William Militare. It appears that Spencer probably participated in the D-Day invasion when the 82nd Airborne parachuted behind enemy lines (Spencer was probably in a glider) and given his unit, I suspect he was also a participant in Market Garden, the largest parachute drop in history. Discharged in December 1945. Graduated from Groton High School in 1940.

416. **Lester Sperry,** US Army, served three years during WWII. Born near Groton in 1914 to Mr. and Mrs. Clarence Sperry.

417. **Henry L. Stange,** US Army, PFC. Killed in action October 9, 1944, in Italy. Stange was a nephew of Mrs. Ben Lorenz of Groton. Son of Conrad Stange, formerly of Groton.

418. **Harold L. Steffen,** US Army, Corporal, returned via troop ship from Korea in March 1952, native of Andover.

419. **Donald C. Stevens,** US Navy, enlisted in January 1952, native of Groton.

420. **Gordon Stone, Dr.,** US Army, served several years during WWII. Graduated from Andover High School.

421. **Glen A. Strom,** US Army, served two years prior to 1948. Born to Charles and Hulda Strom in Groton.

422. **Edwin Sundberg,** US Army, served in North Africa and Italy. While serving as a radio operator for the artillery, he was awarded the Bronze Star for heroic achievement in action on October 10, 1944.

Edwin Sundberg

Joyce Sundling

423. **Joyce Elizabeth Sundling,** US Navy (Waves), served stateside from 1943 through 1945. Graduated from Groton High School in 1938. Mother of Jerry, Bob, and Diane, all graduates of Groton High School.

424. **Jay Swisher**, US Army, 27th Infantry of the 9th Armored Division, European Theater, Battle of the Bulge, Battle at Remagen to capture the Ludendorff Bridge over the Rein into Germany, and the Ardennes. Purple Heart recipient. Bronze Star. Served from 1941 through 1946 with the final rank of First Lieutenant. According to Bill Swisher, Jay did not speak much about the service time. However, Jay did receive seven field promotions (blood stripes—taking the place for wounded or killed men) and during the Battle of the Bulge subsisted on six ration candy bars

Jay Swisher

for ten days. Was wounded when his jeep was hit by German shelling. Swisher woke up on the operating table in inches of his own blood. Received shell fragments in his back and back side. He recuperated from his wounds in England. Jay was a member of the South Dakota State Legislature for two years, starting in 1967, and was South Dakota Secretary of Agriculture from 1988 to 1995. He died in 2008.

425. **Harold Taylor,** US Navy, enlisted in 1943. Member of the Groton American Legion Post #39. His son, Richard and his wife, Judy Taylor live in Groton. Taylor passed away at the Beverly Healthcare Center in 1992.

426. **Boyd H. Tewksbury,** US Army, Sergeant, returned via troop ship from Korea in April 1952, native of Andover.

427. **F. William (Bill) Tewksbury,** US Army, Sergeant, in August 1954 served with 630th Engineers. Son of Mr. and Mrs. C.W. Tewksbury of Andover. A 1947 graduate of Groton High School.

Bill Tewskbury

428. **Darwin D. Thompson,** US Army, drafted in 1945 and discharged in 1946. Attended Groton High School.

429. **Marvin T. Thompson,** US Army, Private, in March 1951, left for Fort Lawton, Washington, to be transferred overseas. Native of Andover.

430. **Robert S. Thompson,** US Army, Signal Corps, discharged because of a back issue. Married to Mary Simonson from Groton.

431. **Norman Thurston**, US Army, Purple Heart recipient, 27th Division, 165th Infantry. Marianas Islands, Gilbert, Marshall, Salomon, Guam, and Saipan. Served in 1941 through 1945. Wounded on Saipan Island.

Norman Thurston

432. **Marvin L. Tjosten,** US Army, Colonel, in February 1964, was awarded the Legion of Merit, one of highest decorations that may be given to military men in peacetime. It was presented to Tjosten by Lieutenant General Charles B. Duff shortly before Tjosten retired in December 1963. Tjosten graduated in 1931 from South Dakota State College and entered the US Army in 1940. His wife is the former Muriel Rasmussen who lived in Putney.

433. **Merrill J. Tolze,** US Navy, promoted to Aviation Machinist's Mate Third Class in 1951. Tolze was stationed at Navy Base at Guantanamo Bay, Cuba, and was a native of Andover.

434. **James (Jim) Torguson**, US Air Force, in 1952, was stationed in Merced, California. Previously stationed in Spokane, Washington, Albuquerque, New Mexico, and Thule, Greenland.

435. **Art Totske,** US Navy, Saipan for two years. Lived in the Groton area after his discharge until his death in 2001.

Art Totske

436. **Norman H. Townsend,** US Army, Private, in June 1956, graduated from the Army's Artillery and Guided Missile School at Fort Sill, Oklahoma. Pierpont High

School graduate in 1953 and entered the Army in November 1955. Son of Mr. and Mrs. H.L. Townsend of Andover.

437. **Arthur Tribble,** in April 1953, returned from serving in Germany, was discharged. Son of Mr. and Mrs. Joe Tribble of Andover.

438. **Merlin Tunby,** US Air Force, in April 1953 completed basic training at Lackland Air Force Base, Texas. Son of Mr. and Mrs. Edward Tunby of Columbia.

439. **Verne Tunby,** graduate of Columbia High School.

440. **Joseph Udelhofen,** veteran of WWII. Raised in Verdon.

441. **LeRoy J. Vetch,** US Marines, Corporal, inducted into Marines in September 1951.
In April 1952 graduated with honors from the radio telegraph operator's course. Assigned to USS *Taconic*, a ship resupplying advance bases and weather stations near the North Pole in September 1952. Son of Mr. and Mrs. Sebastian Vetch of Stratford.

Verne Tunby

442. **Robert Vietmeir,** veteran of WWII. Raised in Hecla/Claremont area until moving to Flandreau in 1979.

443. **Robert Vitense,** US Army, graduated from Columbia High School in 1951.

444. **Clinton Voight,** US Army, received the Victory Occupation Medal (Germany). Graduated from Groton High School in 1944.

445. **Clyde Voss,** US Army, South Dakota National Guard, and served in WWII in the South Pacific. Attended school in Andover.

446. **Donald S. Waage,** was honorably discharged and returned to work for Northwestern Bell/US West in Aberdeen. Graduated from Pierpont High School in 1952. Moved to Groton in 1967.

447. **Jason K. Waage,** US Army, Private in 1951, from Groton. After leave, Waage was assigned to Far Eastern theater of operations. He completed basic training in Fort Riley, Kansas.

448. **Edward Warren Wahlquist,** US Marines, in November 1955, was inducted into the Marines and trained at San Diego, California. Wahlquist was a former resident of St. Paul and moved to Groton prior to entering the service.

449. **Vernie Walter,** US Army, entered US Army after graduating from Groton High School in 1943.

Vernie Walter

450. **Robert L. Washnok,** US Army, Sergeant First Class, in August 1959, was assigned to individual weapons training at Clemson College. Graduate of Groton High School and son of Henry E. Washnok of Groton.

451. **R. S. (Robert) Wegner**, US Navy, Seaman First Class, plane captain, USS *Shipley Bay* in the South Pacific, served

R.S. Wegner

January 1944 through December 1945. Graduate of Groton High School.

452. **Robert Wehde**, US Army, 1953-1955. Graduate of Groton High School.

453. **Duane F. Weifenbach,** US Army, Sergeant First Class, native of Columbia, returned to US Army Hospital at Camp McCoy, Wisconsin. Assigned to Heidelberg, Germany in April 1956. In March 1957, Weifenbach arrived from Heidelberg, Germany, for a 45-day furlough and reported to Fort Riley, Kansas. Served in Heidelberg for three years. May 1959 assigned to VI US Army Corps, Terre Haute, Indiana. Son of Mr. and Mrs. Henry Weifenbach of Columbia.

Robert Wehde

454. **Edward Weifenbach,** US Army, Sergeant, entered the Army on November 1, 1951, and received his discharge from the Army at Camp Carson, Colorado, in September 1953. Son of Mr. and Mrs. Henry Weifenbach of Columbia.

455. **Gerald Weifenbach,** US Army, Private First Class, returned to Camp Chaffee, Alaska, in August 1955 after spending a furlough with parents, Mr. and Mrs. Henry Weifenbach of Columbia. In April 1956, Weifenbach arrived in Germany where he served with the 25th AAA Battalion, near Heidelberg, Germany. In July 1956, Gerald took part in a field training test held by the 25th Anti-Aircraft Battalion. Weifenbach was a clerk in Battery C. Graduated in 1955 from Columbia

High School. In March 1959, Gerald returned to Columbia after being discharged from the Army after serving for three years in Germany.

456. **Martin H. Weismantle,** US Air Force, Private in 1951. Son of Mr. and Mrs. William Weismantel of Columbia. Correct spelling of Martin's name is **Weismantel**. Clerk typist during induction misspelled name, as a result Martin's name for entire tour of duty was Weismantle.

Martin Weismantle

457. **Albert D. Wellman,** US Army, veteran of WWII. Moved to Andover in 1964.

458. **Marvin Werr,** US Navy, WWII, graduate of Columbia High School.

459. **John Westby**, US Army, 1st Infantry Division, Pusan, Korea, from 1946 through 1947.

460. **Norman Widney,** US Army, in August 1955, was given discharge after serving in Germany and France. Son of A.E. Widney of Andover.

461. **Norman Widvey,** US Army, enlisted in December 1953, native of Andover.

462. **Gerald M. Wilber,** US Navy, served June 1941 to December 1945. Retired and moved to Ferney in 1979.

463. **Robert Roy Williams,** US Marine, Private, underwent basic training in October 1952. Graduated from Turton High School and the son of Mr. and Mrs. Roy Williams of Turton.

464. **Erwin Wilmsen,** veteran of WWII. Born in Groton in 1910 and member of the American Legion at Groton. Resident of the Groton/Andover area all his life.

465. **Robert A. (Bob) Winegar,** US Air Force, Airman Second Class, signed up for the Air Force just prior to graduation from Bonilla High School in May 1953. Entered Air Force in August 1953 and served through July 1957. Attended radio school at Scott Air Force Base, Illinois. Was stationed in Wiesbaden, Germany, for three years. Winegar's wife is Ann Knickrehm, a 1958 graduate of Groton High School. Residents of Groton and member of Groton American Legion Club and lifetime member of the VFW.

Bob Winegar

466. **Leonard Witt,** US Army Air Corps, veteran of WWII. Moved to Groton in 1946 and left in 1959.

467. **James L. Wockenfuss,** US Army, Master Sergeant (E8) in 1951. In 1951, completed a seven-year tour in Germany. In January 1951 named outstanding non-commissioned officer at the engineer depot in Hanau, Germany. Son of Mrs. Mabel Wockenfuss of Columbia.

468. **Jerome Wright,** US Army, graduated in 1954 from Columbia High School.

469. **Lester Yeske,** US Army, Private, served from 1944 through 1946, in Germany. Medals awarded include Army of Occupation and EAMET. Native of Columbia.

470. **Jeron Zastrow,** US Army, graduated from Columbia High School in 1952.

471. **Dwight Zeller,** US Army, served in the South Pacific.

472. **Richard Zimney,** US Air Force, entered service in 1951 and served in Philippine Islands during the Korean War. Graduated from Groton High School in 1949.

473. **Robert Zoellner,** US Army. Graduated from Groton High School.

Richard Zimney

1956 through 1961

1. **Ronald Adler,** US Army, Private First Class, member of 716th Army Reserve Unit activated in August 1961 and a graduate of Groton High School.

2. **George Amsden,** US Marines, Private First Class, in September 1958, enlisted and received basic training at San Diego, California. In September 1959, arrived at Naha, Okinawa, with the First Battalion, Fifth Marine Regiment for 15 months of duty. A 1958 graduate of Groton High School and son of Mr. and Mrs. George Amsden of Groton.

3. **Gerald L. Barrie,** US Navy, Ship's Serviceman Second Class, in October 1959, participated in training in six-man, pararescue teams which provide search and rescue capability. In November 1960, Barrie arrived in the Antarctic to participate in the Navy's 1961 Operation Deep Freeze. Son of Mr. and Mrs. Lawrence Barrie of Turton.

4. **James P. Barrie,** US Army, Private, in June 1959 completed advanced individual heavy weapon training at Fort Ord, California. 1954 graduate of Turton High School. Son of Peter Barrie of Turton.

5. **Joseph A. Barrie,** US Army, Private, in June 1958, completed an eight-week automotive maintenance course at Fort Chaffee, AR. 1957 graduate of Doland

High School and son of Mr. and Mrs. Lawrence Barrie of Turton.

6. **Bob O. Berg,** US Marines, Private, in May 1959, returned to Camp Pendleton, California, after spending 14-day furlough with his parents, Mr. and Mrs. Joe Berg of Verdon. In June 1959, transferred to Okinawa for overseas duty and assigned to 3rd Marine Division to serve 15 months.

7. **John T. Berry,** US Army, 2nd Lieutenant, in July 1958, ended a six-week summer camp at Fort Riley, Kansas, under the Reserve Officer Training Corps Program of South Dakota State University. In June 1960, completed the eight-week officer basic course at the Army Armor School, Fort Knox, Kentucky. Berry received training in the duties of a platoon leader in a tank reconnaissance company. Graduate of the University of South Dakota. Son of Mr. and Mrs. N.H. Berry of Groton.

8. **Kenneth L. Campbell,** US Marines, Private First Class, enlisted in September 1958 and received basic training at San Diego, California. In February 1959, was scheduled to finish four weeks of individual combat training at Marine Corps Base, Camp Pendleton, California. 1958 graduate of Groton High School. Son of Mr. and Mrs. W. F. Campbell of Groton.

9. **Gordon Cavanaugh,** US Air Force, Staff Sergeant, in August 1960, transferred to Grand Forks Air Force Base. Son of Mrs. Pearl Cavanaugh of Andover.

10. **Bernard (Tiny) W. Christenson,** US Army, Specialist 4, in December 1958, completed basic training at Fort Carson, Colorado. Served in Panama. Son of Mr. and Mrs. Oscar Christenson, Britton. Brother of Jean Schaller and Marian Raines of Groton.

Tiny Christenson

11. **Rollin Christenson,** US Army, Specialist 4, in March 1957, graduated from the liquid oxygen generation course at the Army's Engineer School, Fort Belvoir, Virginia. Entered the Army in November 1956 and completed basic training at Fort Chaffee, Alaska. Son of Mr. and Mrs. Oscar Christenson, Britton, and brother of Jean Schaller and Marian Raines of Groton.

Rollin Christenson

12. **Glenn N. Cooper, Luverne L. Strom, James E. Johnson,** in September 1961, left for induction into the armed services.

13. **Anthony Daly,** US Army, 1957 graduate of Columbia High School.

Glenn N. Cooper

14. **Robert Davis,** US Air Force, 1959 graduate of Columbia High School.

15. **Donald W. DeVries,** US Army, Private, in November 1956, received advanced infantry training with the 4th Division at Fort Lewis, Washington. A 1950 graduate of Pierpont High School and the son of Mr. and Mrs. Thomas DeVries of Andover.

16. **Dave Doeringsfeld,** no information available.

17. **Lawrence Dolney**, US Army, South Dakota National Guard, Alaska.

18. **James Donovan,** US Army, Private, in October 1960, completed basic training at Fort Hood, Texas. Assigned to Fort Sill, Oklahoma, after a 10-day leave with his parents, Mr. and Mrs. Jerry Donovan of Groton.

19. **Richard Donovan,** US Army, served from 1958 through 1959. Attached to a medical unit in Frankfurt, Germany. Played on one of the US Army baseball teams. He was one of two players on the team that did not have pro-baseball experience. Richard taught and coached in the Groton High School for 18 years and returned in 1995 to retire in Groton.

20. **Kent Elliott,** US Army, 1956 graduate of Columbia High School.

21. **Harlan E. Ellis,** US Navy, Seaman Apprentice, in August 1956, graduated from Naval Training Center, Great Lakes, Illinois, after nine weeks of basic training. Assigned to Great Lakes for advanced training after leave with his parents, Mr. and Mrs. Cyril Ellis of Columbia.

22. **Dean Emmen,** US Air Force, in February 1959 enlisted in Air Force and underwent basic training in Texas. In November 1959, completed 26 weeks of radio intercept school and was assigned to San Antonio, Texas, for an additional eight weeks of advanced schooling. Son of Mr. and Mrs. Hans Emmen of Andover.

23. **James Feist,** US Army, in 1960s.

24. **Wayne Felix,** US Army, 1957 graduate of Columbia High School.

25. **Warren Felix,** US Army, 1957 graduate of Columbia High School.

26. **James E. Fortin,** US Marines, Sergeant, in March 1957, arrived at the home of Mr. and Mrs. Victor Fortin of Turton, for a 14-day furlough. In December 1958, served in El Toro Marine Corps Air Station, Santa Ana, California. In October 1958, served with the Marine Fighter Squadron 314 of Marine Aircraft Group 11. The group was assigned as a security force for Taiwan. In December 1959, served with Third Marine Aircraft Wing at El Toro Marine Corps Air Station, Santa Ana, California.

27. **Roger A. Fortin,** US Navy, in December 1960, graduated from recruit training at the Naval Training Center, San Diego, California. Son of Mr. and Mrs. Victor Fortin of Turton.

28. **Robert Gooding,** US Air Force, in October 1957 entered the Air Force and traveled to Texas where he received training. Son of Mr. and Mrs. Harold Gooding of Andover.

29. **Clifford S. Hammond,** US Air Force, Airman, in February 1958 assigned to 3275th Technical Training Group at Lackland Air Force Base, Texas, to undergo basic air police training. Son of Mrs. Clifford Hammond of Groton.

30. **Clarence Hannon**, US Army, served in Germany in 1956. Graduated from Andover High School in 1951.

31. **Arlis Hanson,** US Army, 1956 graduate of Columbia High School.

32. **George M. Hansen,** US Navy, Seaman Recruit, in December 1956, enlisted in the Navy at the Aberdeen recruiting substation. He was assigned to Great Lakes Naval Training Center, Illinois, for nine weeks of recruit training. Graduated from Stratford High School. Son of Mr. and Mrs. George Hanson of Stratford.
George Hansen

33. **Larry Laverne Hanson,** US Army, Private, member of 716th Army Reserve Unit, was activated in August 1961. Graduated from Columbia High School in 1955.

34. **Merle Hanson**, US Army. Purchased Groton Truck Center and Trail Chevrolet.

35. **Gary Heitmann,** US Air Force Reserve, served from 1956 through 1967, 119th Fighter Wing in Fargo, North Dakota. Graduate of Britton High School and retired in Groton.
Gary Heitmann

36. **Terry Dean Hochhalter,** US Army, Private, member of 716th Army Reserve Unit, was activated in August 1961. Native of Columbia.

37. **Harwood H. Hoeft,** US Army, 2nd Lieutenant, in December 1959, completed the 10-week officer

rotary-wing qualification course. Entered service in February 1959. Son of Mr. and Mrs. Henry J. Hoeft of Stratford.

38. **Henry J. Hoeft,** US Air Force, Airman Second Class, in March 1961, was assigned to US Air Force Hospital, Travis Air Force Base, California. Son of Mr. and Mrs. Harrie G. Hoeft of Stratford.

39. **Howard Hoeft**, US Air Force, Aviator, 1959.

40. **Leon E. Howe,** US Navy, Machinist's Mate First Class, in February 1959, served aboard USS *Cavalier*, operating out of Long Beach, California. Son of Mrs. Clifford Howe of Houghton.

41. **Thomas E. Howell,** US Army, Private, member of 716th Army Reserve Unit activated in August 1961, native of Columbia.

42. **Terrence C. Hubbard,** US Naval Academy, Midshipmen First Class, in December 1956, was home with his parents, Mr. and Mrs. Ronald Hubbard of Groton, for Christmas leave. Entered US Naval Academy in June 1956. Received his appointment through an academic examination through the Naval Reserve service training program. In August 1958, Hubbard entered a three-week Air Indoctrination Course at Naval Air Station Pensacola, Florida.

43. **Kenneth R. Johnson,** US Air Force, Airman Second Class, arrived in Groton in June 1958 to spend a 30-day leave with relatives and friends.

44. **Everett Jones,** US Army, in January 1958, spent a 30-day leave with his parents, Mr. and Mrs. Russell Jones of Groton. At expiration of leave, Jones returned to Fort Benning, Georgia, and left for Germany in March 1958.

Everett Jones

45. **Clayton Jones,** US Army, Specialist Third Class, in December 1957, was on leave with his parents, Mr. and Mrs. Russell Jones of Groton. Assigned to Fort Belvoir, Virginia, to attend specialist's school after expiration of the leave.

46. **Larry R. Karlen,** US Marines, 2nd Lieutenant, in June 1960, Karlen was one of 190 graduates of the Officer Candidate School, Quantico, Virginia. He attended a 26-week basic school at Quantico for newly commissioned officers. Graduate of Kansas State University and the son of Mr. and Mrs. Larry R. Karlen of Columbia.

47. **Arnold E. Klemensen,** US Air Force, served in England for four years after he graduated from Conde High School in 1956. Born in Verdon. Lived in Brown County most of his life.

48. **Allan R. Kenny,** US Army, Private, in October 1960, completed the supply specialist course at Fort Leonard Wood, Missouri. Son of Mr. and Mrs. George H. Kenny of Houghton.

49. **Bernie Klapperich,** US Army, Private, in March 1957, returned to Fort Ord, California, after a furlough with his parents, Mr. and Mrs. Leon Klapperich of Turton.

50. **Richard Kluge,** US Navy, from 1954 to 1957. In 1977, moved to rural Groton.

51. **Eugene H. Kramp,** US Navy, Lieutenant Commander, in October 1958, entered helicopter training at Helicopter Training Group, Ellyson Field, Pensacola, Florida. Husband of former Ms. Olive L. Kramer of Andover.

52. **Lyle Kranzler,** US Army, Private, in January 1957, left for induction in the Army at Fort Ord, California, for basic training. His wife, the former Kay Raap of Andover resided at the Paul Kranzler home while he was in the service. In February 1959, arrived in Andover area to visit family and friends after being discharged from the Army.

53. **Donald Krege,** US Army, paratrooper, 1956 graduate of Columbia High School.

54. **Richard O. Kroll,** US Army, Private First Class, member of H&S Company, US Army Garrison in Verdun, France. Entered the Army in February 1956. His parents live in Andover.

55. **Gary L. Krueger,** US Army, Private, in May 1958, passed an Army code intelligence test and left for Fort Gordon, Georgia, after his basic training at Fort Leonard Wood, Missouri. In October 1958, completed his course at the Army Code Intelligence School, Fort Gordon, Georgia. Son of Mr. and Mrs. Alex P. Krueger of Groton.

56. **Robert A. Kruse,** US Army, Private, in September 1959, completed eight weeks of basic training at Fort Carson, Colorado, and was assigned to Fort Gordon, Georgia, for six months of schooling in radar and radio communications. In November 1959, completed the eight-week radio carrier operation course at Fort Gordon, Georgia. 1957 graduate of Columbia High School. Son of Mrs. Lillian Kruse of Columbia.

57. **John A. LaBrie,** US Army National Guard, in November 1959, completed six months active duty and accepted a position as an electrical engineer with Boeing Aircraft in Seattle, Washington. Graduate of Turton High School and South Dakota State College. Member of National Guard of Seattle, Washington. Son of Mr. and Mrs. Victor LaBrie of Turton.

58. **Lynn C. LaBrie,** US Navy, Seaman Second Class, in May 1960, returned aboard destroyer, USS *Cone*, after a seven-month tour of duty with the Sixth Fleet in the Mediterranean. Besides participating in various operational exercises, the Cone and crew visited Spain, France, Italy, and Greece. Son of Mr. and Mrs. Leon C. LaBrie of Turton.

59. **Allen L. Larson**, US Army, Private First Class, in March 1959, completed basic training at Fort Leonard Wood, Missouri. Arrived overseas (Germany) in August 1960. Graduated from Groton High School in 1954 and son of Mr. and Mrs. Lawrence T. Larson of Aberdeen.

60. **Gary Lenling**, South Dakota Nation Guard.

61. **Ralph R. Lilly,** US Air Force, in October 1956, was sworn into the Air Force at the Sioux Falls Recruiting Center. Son of Mr. and Mrs. Elmer Lilly of Andover.

62. **Jerauld M. Locken,** US Navy, in October 1956, was appointed master-at-arms of his recruit company at Great Lakes Training Center, Illinois. Son of Mr. and Mrs. John C. Locken of Stratford.

63. **Bernard J. Mallett,** US Army, Specialist 4, in July 1960, returned to Fort Lewis, Washington, after a 30-day furlough with his parents, Mr. and Mrs. Harold Mallett of Chelsea, SD. Returned from a year in Korea where he was with the 1st Cavalry Division Honor Guard. Graduate of Andover High School and lived in Andover prior to his enlistment.

64. **Jerry Mannie,** US Air Force, Airman Third Class, in March 1957, left for an assignment to an air force base in Greenland. Son of Mr. and Mrs. Henry Mannie of Turton.

65. **Bertell Martin**, South Dakota National Guard.

66. **Lloyd Martin,** US Air Force, Airman Second Class, in January 1960, returned to Fort Bragg, North Carolina, after several days with his parents, Mr. and Mrs. Edward E. Martin of Andover.

67. **Marilyn Martin,** US Air Force, Women's Air Force, in February 1959, took basic training at Lackland Air Force Base in Texas. Daughter of Mrs. Dorothy Martin of Groton.

68. **Robert J. Martin,** US Army, Private, in January 1958, completed basic training under the Reserve Forces Act Program at Fort Leonard Wood, Missouri. Son of Mr. and Mrs. Edward E. Martin of Andover.

69. **George E. Mathieu,** US Navy, Seaman Recruit, in July 1958, completed recruit training at the Naval Training Center, Great Lakes, Illinois. Son of Mr. and Mrs. George A. Mathieu of Stratford.

70. **Charles Alvin Meister,** US Navy, Seaman Recruit, in April 1956, enlisted at the Aberdeen recruiting substation, and was assigned to Great Lakes Naval Training Station, Illinois. In January 1958, served aboard USS *Salem*, a heavy cruiser with the 6th Fleet in the Mediterranean. In September 1958, Meister visited Barcelona, Spain, while serving aboard USS *Salem*. Son of Mr. and Mrs. Erwin Meister of Groton.

71. **Mervyn Meister,** US Army, Private, in February 1958, returned to Fort Riley, Kansas, after a 30-day leave with his parents, Mr. and Mrs. Erwin Meister of Groton. In November 1960, Meister returned home from Hawaii, was discharged, and left for Rapid City, SD, to work with the Dakota Lime and Brick Company.

72. **Vance Edward Miller, Jr.,** graduated first in his class at Naval Officer Candidate School and was assigned to San Francisco Naval Shipyard in 1955. Miller was born in Groton and a graduate of Groton High School.

Vance Miller

73. **William Mohn,** US Air Force, in August 1956, enlisted in the Air Force and reported to Parks Air Force Base in California. Son of Mrs. Gertrude Mohn of Andover.

74. **Donald L. Morehouse,** US Navy, Seaman, in November 1961, was scheduled to be promoted while serving in the Western Pacific aboard the 7th Fleet Troop Transport, USS *George Clymer.* Son of Mr. and Mrs. Lloyd Morehouse of Andover.

75. **Edward Neff,** South Dakota National Guard, 1957.

76. **Carrol (Spike) Nehls**, US Marines.

77. **John Nissen,** US Air Force, in January 1959, reported to Austin, Texas, for electrical engineering instructions after 30-day leave with his parents, Mr. and Mrs. Hans Nissen of Groton.

78. **Gary L. Olson,** US Army, Private First Class, in February 1958, participated in maneuvers with the 29th Infantry at Fort Greely, Alaska. Entered the Army in October 1956 and graduated from Columbia High School in 1956. Son of Mr. and Mrs. Leonard Olson of Bath. Wife, Linda, resided in Columbia.

79. **Donald L. Pence,** US Army, Specialist 4, in October 1958, was assigned to 530th Engineer Company, Schwetzingen, Germany. 1953 graduate of Columbia High School and the son of Mr. and Mrs. Robert M. Pence of Columbia.

80. **James R. Pigors,** US Army, Private, in November 1956, graduated with honors from vehicle repairman course

at the Army's European Ordinance School in Fuessen, Germany. Returned to his regular assignment with the 41st Tank Battalion, Company C. Pigors entered the Army in February 1956 and received basic training at Fort Carson, Colorado. Pigors was discharged in 1962. Graduated from Groton High School in 1951. Son of Mr. and Mrs. Arthur O. Pigors of Andover.

81. **Nancy Pulfrey,** US Navy, Waves, in May 1956, enlisted at the Aberdeen Recruiting Substation, assigned to Bainbridge, MA Naval Station for 11 weeks of recruit training. Daughter of Mrs. Mary Pulfrey of Houghton. Graduate of Hecla High School.

82. **Larry D. Rabine,** US Marines, Private, in May 1960, completed four weeks of individual combat training at the Marine Corps Base, Camp Pendleton, California. In November 1960, participated in amphibious landing exercises while serving with the First Marine Division's Battalion Landing Team at Camp Pendleton, California. Son of Mr. and Mrs. Mike Rabine of Andover.

83. **Robert E. Richards,** US Army, Private First Class, in March 1958, arrived in Munich, Germany as a member of the 11th Airborne Division. In June 1958, assigned to 596th Transportation Company in Augsburg, Germany as a training specialist. Son of Mr. and Mrs. Roy A. Richards of Groton.

84. **Verl A. Ringgenberg**, US Navy, Command Master Chief (Ret), South Dakota National Guard Jan 1955 through June 1956, US Navy boot camp Treasure Island CA, August 1956 through February 1957.

Verl A. Ringgenberg

Retired in 1974 and transferred to Fleet Reserve. Served aboard USS *Hale*, USS *Raymond*, USS *Delong*, and USS *Decatur* as well as various instructor assignments. In the fall of 1956 there were five Columbia grads stationed within the San Francisco Bay area - all Navy. **Don Dennert** - Seaplane Tender; **Harly Kruse** - Alameda Naval Air Station; **RayDean Schliebe** - Radar Picket; and **Bob Vitense and Verl Ringgenberg** - APA at Hunters Point. Spent a lot of time with Bob and his wife Kathy as they lived on base at Hunter Point. Many weekends of cards and board games kept me out of trouble

85. **Dean W. Ringgenberg,** US Air Force, Airman, in December 1959, completed initial course of Air Force basic training. Selected to attend the technical training course for aircraft and missile maintenance at Sheppard Air Force Base, Texas. A 1959 graduate of Columbia High School and son of Mr. and Mrs. Arthur Ringgenberg of Columbia.

86. **John D. Rock,** US Army, Private, in March 1959, graduated from basic training at Fort Leonard Wood, Missouri. Member of the Minnesota National Guard from 1958 to 1960. Son of Mr. and Mrs. William H. Rock of Groton.

87. **Gary Sieber,** US Army, 1956 graduate of Columbia High School.

88. **Harlowe E. Sombke,** US Navy, Chief Engineer, in February 1961, graduated from the Electrician's Mate School, Naval Training Center, Great Lakes, Illinois. Son of Mr. and Mrs. Clarence C. Sombke of Verdon.

89. **Clayton Sternhagen**, US Army, 1956. Spent most of his time in the Washington DC area with a Nike missile unit. Moved to Groton in 1961.

90. **Owen E. Swenson,** US Air Force, Airman Second Class, in January 1960, was promoted to the grade of Airman Second Class. Assigned to 376 Armament Squadron, Lockbourne Air Force Base, Ohio. Son of Mr. and Mrs. Oscar Swenson of Groton. Swenson is a 1956 graduate of Aberdeen High School.

Roland Tullis

91. **Roland Tullis,** US Army, Germany. 1956 graduate of Groton High School.

92. **Delwin Albert Tullis,** South Dakota National Guard, 1957 graduate of Groton High School.

93. **Forest Vitense,** US Navy, in April 1956, enlisted at the Aberdeen Recruiting Substation, assigned to Great Lakes Naval Training Station, Illinois. Son of Mr. and Mrs. Rudy Vitense of Columbia. A 1955 graduate of Columbia High School.

94. **John (Jack) Walter,** US Army, stationed in the DMZ in the 1950s. A 1953 graduate of Groton High School.

95. **Allan Weismantel,** US Air Force, 1959 to 1963, stationed at Webb Air Force Base, Big Spring, TX. Assigned to the Academics section, where he oversaw all the pilot training students' academic records. 1957 graduate of Columbia High School.

Allan Weismantel

96. **Howard O. Wheelock, Jr.,** US Navy, Radioman Third Class, in January 1961, served aboard USS *Kawishiwi* operating out of Pearl Harbor, Hawaii. Son of Mr. and Mrs. H.O. Wheelock Sr. of Putney.

97. **Billie Willis,** US Navy, in March 1958, was on leave in Andover. At expiration of leave, Willis reported back to either a school station or ships in the fleet.

98. **Roy Wood,** US Army, Private, entered the Army in September 1956 and was assigned at Camp Chaffee, Alaska, Fort Carson, Colorado, and Fort Ord, California, where he received additional infantry training. Son of Mrs. Myrtle Wood of Aberdeen. Visited friends and relatives in December 1956 on a holiday furlough in Stratford and Aberdeen.

99. **Jerome D. Wright,** US Army, Private, in June 1959, completed the final phase of his six months active military training under the Reserve Forces Act Program at Fort Sill, Oklahoma. Son of Mrs. Florence Wright of Houghton. A 1954 graduate of Columbia High School.

100. **Robert L. Zastrow,** US Army, Private, in December 1956, spent a 14-day furlough with his parents, Mr. and Mrs. Helmuth Zastrow of Columbia. Attended a 25-week school in radio installation and maintenance at Signal Corps School. Received basic training in Fort Carson, Colorado.

101. **Nickolas J. Zimmerman,** US Air Force, Private, in October 1956, sworn into the Air Force at the Sioux Falls Recruiting Center. In December 1956, spent a furlough with his parents, Mr. and Mrs. Bernard

Zimmerman of Andover. His next assignment was at the Air Force Station, Finley, North Dakota.

102. **Donald P. Zimmerman,** US Army, Private, in October 1960, was assigned to Dugway Proving Grounds, Dugway, Utah, upon completing basic combat training at Fort Hood, Texas. Son of Mr. and Mrs. Bernard Zimmerman of Andover.

The Groton American Legion has provided me a list of service members or individuals associated with military service members that are buried in the Groton Cemetery as well as veterans buried in Ferney, Verdon, Huffton, Augustana, James, and Bates Scotland. Those individuals are listed below. I suspect that most are veterans of WWI, WWII, and some from later years.

A: ABELN Edward; ADAMS, F.S.; ALBERT, John; AMSDEN, Lyman; ARNDT, Fred and Carl; ARCHER, Bartley; ANDERSON, Carl; and AHERN, Charles.

B: BERG, George; BOEHMER, Walter; BENNET, Alfred; BARBER, Eugene; BATES, Issack; BLOCK, Lowell; BAKER, Richard; BELDEN, Herbert; BLACKMUN, Bert; BENNETT, Henry; BOWERS, Malverm; BINGHAM, Carrol; BLAIR, Robert; BUFFINGTON, Rodney; BROTT, S.F.; BENZ, Paul; BREDBERG, Neil; BRISTOL, Harley Pop; and BROWN, Hildegarde B.

C: CASSELS, Leon and Eugene; CAIN, Joe; CLEMENSEN, Danial; CAMPBELL, Dwight Jr.; CUTLER, Verl; CURRY, J.W.; COOK, S.W.; COLE, L.T. and Emmet; and CURRY, William.

D: DAVIDSON, Carl and Gust; DOBSON, H.C.; DOMBROWE, Oscar; DOBBERPUHL, Edwin; DYE, Rahel Haire and Clarence "C.C."; DICKERSON, B.F.; DICKENS, George; DIXON, Jesse; and DECAMP, James.

E: ESKE, Louis; ERICKSON, Kenneth.

F: FRY, John P., James, and John; FESER, Harold; FULLER, FANGEN, Hans; FERGUSON, Duane; FELLOWS, Isaac; and FELLER, Sammual J.

G: GIBBS, H.P. and John; GEFFRE, Clemens; GELYARD, Hjalmer; GRAMS, Louis; and GOULD, William F.

H: HATTON, John and David; HEATH, M.A.; HILTON, S.H.; HAMILTON, Roy; HARMS, Robert; HAIRE Robert; HAGIN, James W; HANSON, Royal; HEIT, John; HEWETT, Norman; HEMAN, Loren; HURD, James A.; HOFFMAN, Ronald; HENIHAN Ulic; Hall, Johns S.; HAGEN, Darrel K.; HUFFMAN, Henry; HOSTETTER, Enos; HARVEY, Fred L.; and HOLDER, John.

I: IVES, Howard.

J: JOHNSON, James, John J., William A., Myron, Ed, and Herb; JORGENSON, DeWayne; JONES, Howard; and JOHNKE, Charles.

K: KUEHNERT, Herman; KEPKE, John; Kaufman, Joe; KARNOPP, Herman; KLUDT, Harold; KROLL, Jake; KNUDSEN, Elmer; KLEMENSON, Arnold; and KRUEGAR, Paul "Lefty."

L: LEAK, James; LEONHART, Delbert; LOWARY, Loy; LARSON, Henry, and Lars; LYONS, Zack; LIETZ, Charles; LORENZ, James; and LIEBEL, Carl.

M: MESSER, C.E.; MEREDITH, Earl; MURRAY, James; MICKO, Bradley; MUSEL, Gervis Fred; MERENESS, George; MCFARLANE, Walter; MASKE, William; MEHAFFEY, Robert and Arthur; MUELLER, Earl; MAY, Marvin; MALLETT, Elliot; MCGEE, Fred and Frank; MATTHEWS, Dustan; MUTH, Frank; and MURRAY, James and John.

N: NAEVE, LaVerne; NEHLS, Fred, John "Jack," and Raloh; and NIETERT, John.

O: ODLAND, Ernes and Winston; OTTO, Kenneth, Joel, Earl, and Florence; OLSON, Robert; and OVIATT, Anton.

P: PAETZNICK, William J., Alfred, and Oscar; PAETH, Ed and Arthur; PETERSON, Fred; PARKER, J.J.; Paulson, Joseph M.; PAEPKE, Hubert; PERKINS, Carl; PAVEK, S. and James; PULFREY, Gary R., and Myrna; POLIERE, Louis Raymond; PIERSON, Frank, George and Duane; PLATT, Soloman; and PIGORS, Berthold A., Alfred, and Carl.

Q: QUANDAHL, Olaf B.

R: ROCK, William, and Art; RADKE, Arthur; ROGERS, Margaret; RATHBUM, Chas; ROSENBERG, Robert; RITTER, Isaac; ROBINSON, T.J.; RIX, Floyd; RAECKE, Helen; and RICHMOND, Robert.

S: SNYDER, Robert; SPILLOWAY, Loyal; SAMMUEL, Harry; SNELL, Chas.; SMITH, F.C.; SAMUELSON, Ed; SCHALLER, William and Walter; SPILMAHER, William; SCHULTZ, Edward; STANGE, William; SIPPEL, Blaine and Orlyin; SLATER, James; SCHINKEL, Herman; SLETTEN, Robert; and SEVERSON, Richard.

T: TEWKSBURY, Clarence; TUTHILL, Vernon; THEDE, Pellman and John; and TRAYLOR, Terry.

V: VOY, August; Van Riper, J.H. and W.L.; VOLK, Joe E.; VOLD, Leland; and VEITSCH, William.

W: WEAVER, Vance; WHITEAKER, John; WOOD, William; WATKINS, Ernest; WILLIAMS, Joe; WOKENFUSS, B. and Henry; WILLSEY, Lewis; and WILBURG, Oliver.

Z: ZOELLNER, Otto, and Fred.

Buried at Sea: INSLEY, Verne

Summary of Military Activities:

Number of young men and women that served

WWII and the Korean War—1940 through 1955: **475**

1956 through 1961: **104**

Vietnam Era (1962 through 1975): **139**

South Vietnam: **53**

Men that died from combat related injuries

WWII and Korean War:

Clifford Hall, Columbia High School graduate.

Wallace Karnopp, US Navy, 1943 Groton High School graduate, lost at sea.

Donald Knapp, US Marine, son of Mr. and Mrs. Carl Knapp of Groton.

Raymond Lilly, US Army, native of Andover.

Robert Podoll, US Army, native of Westport/Columbia.

Marvin Schliebe, US Navy, died at sea, Aberdeen, married to Goldie Bernice Meyer of Groton.

Henry Stange, US Army, Groton, son of Conrad Stange formerly of Groton.

Charles Fuller, US Navy, 1935 Groton High School graduate.

Alfred Breitkreutz, US Air Force, shot down by a MIG over Korea in 1952, native of Groton.

There were approximately 416,800 US casualties during WWII. Of those, 15,764 were from the state of South Dakota. Only five states exceeded that number: New Jersey, Oklahoma, Hawaii, Arizona, and North Carolina.

South Vietnam:

William E. Pasch, US Army, Groton – 1968.

Roger Sletten Cameron, US Army, Pierpont – 1968.

Ronald Clifford Dexter, US Marines, Milbank – 1966.

Robert Gene Fortin, US Army, Turton – 1971.

Charles Maury Hallstrom, US Army, Webster – 1970.

Lanny Ray Krage, US Marines, Columbia – 1967.

Bernhardt W. (Pee Wee) Miller, US Army, Groton – 1967.

Donald Raymond Sandve, US Army, Langford – 1966.

Curtis Leland Williams, US Army, Webster – 1971.

Donald Protas – Groton – Cancer from Agent Orange.

Robert Sieber – Columbia – Cancer from Agent Orange.

Purple Heart Recipients (excluding those who died in combat):

LaVerne Debilzan—South Vietnam.

Larry Ragels—South Vietnam.

Henry Carlson—WWII.

Erwin G. Emmen—WWII.

Maurice Hitchcock—WWII.

Juel Kolbo—WWII.

Art Krage – WWII.

Emil Krage—WWII.

Darwin R. Lovell—Korean War.

Homer Mydland—WWII.

Herman Nilsson—WWII.

Reuban Paul—WWII.

DeWain Peterson—WWII.

Lloyd Schlichting—WWII.

Robert Schuelke—WWII.

Jay Swisher—WWII.

Norman Thurston—WWII.

Thomas (Chick) Blair—WWII.

Career Service Members:

Keith Baggett, US Air Force.

James Baldry, US Army/US Navy, Groton.

Robert Dauwen, US Army, Andover.

Denny Davis, US Navy/Army National Guard, Groton.

Paul Karst, US Army, Groton.

Chuck Lowary (Lieutenant Colonel Retired), US Air Force, Groton High School Class of 1965.

Ron Mielke (Brigadier General Retired), SD National Guard, Groton High School Class of 1960.

Anton Meyer, US Army, Andover.

Berwyn Place (Colonel Retired), US Army.

Robert E. Rystrom (Lieutenant Colonel Retired), Columbia High School graduate.

Freddie Robinson (Warrant Officer Retired), US Army, Stratford/Warner.

Bruce T. Schoonover, US Army, Barnard/Columbia.

Alan E. Wockenfuss (Lieutenant Colonel Retired).

Emil H. Dobberpfuhl, US Air Force, Groton.

Stephen Dresbach (Lieutenant Colonel Retired), Groton High School Class of 1962.

Dennis Furman, South Dakota National Guard.

Donald Helmer (Colonel Retired), US Air Force, Andover High School Class of 1949.

Owen Jones (Lieutenant Colonel Retired), US Army, Groton High School Class of 1971.

Delton S. Feller, US Navy, Groton High School Class of 1927.

Raymond H. Jones, US Air Corps/Air Force Reserve, Hecla High School Class of 1933.

Kenneth V. Karnopp, US Navy, raised and attended two years of high school in Andover.

Marvin D. Kluck (Lieutenant Commander), US Navy, Columbia.

Charles Lapham, US Air Force, Andover High School Class of 1949.

Gerald Meister, US Army.

Arthur E. Mills, US Army, Andover.

J.F. Sherman, US Army, married to Jessie V. Rix from Groton in 1923.

Orville Simonson, US Army, Groton High School Class of 1940.

Marvin L. Tjosten, spouse of Muriel Rasmussen of Putney.

Bob Karlan (Colonel Retired) US National Guard, Columbia and Aberdeen High Schools.

Brad Pigors, US Air Force, Groton High School Class of 1968.

Greg Von Wald (Lieutenant Colonel Retired), US Marines, Groton High School Class of 1967.

David Hosley (Major Retired), US Army, Groton High School Class of 1971.

Charles Lavern Ahern, US Air Force, Groton High School Class of 1943.

Norman Anderson, US Navy, Pierpont.

Charles Barthle (Colonel Retired), US Army, Groton High School Class of 1936.

A difficult issue associated with growing up in the small towns or farms in South Dakota related to job opportunities for young people. It used to be said that South Dakota's biggest export was college-educated young people. If you did not have a large or successful small farm or a business to come home to, opportunities were very limited. To assume that so many men and women entered or stayed in the military because of patriotic feelings is probably an oversimplification. More likely that the best chance for future success was staying in the military and making a career of it or utilizing the GI benefits to get a college education.

Women Who Served:

Kaye P. Gooding, US Army Women's Army Corps, Andover.

Lynette M. Olson, US Navy Waves, Columbia.

Jeannette Blader (Reid), US Navy Waves, Groton High School Class of 1940.

Mercedes Kelly (Julson), US Navy Waves, Andover and Groton school teacher for over 42 years.

Lois Carson Knecht, US Navy Nurse Corps, Houghton.

Marilyn Martin, US Air Force, Groton.

Diana Morehouse, US Marines, Andover.

Clara Ruden (Rix), US Army Women's Army Corps, Groton.

Kathy Shore, US Navy Waves, Columbia High School Class of 1948.

Joyce Elizabeth Sundling, US Navy Waves, Groton.

Nancy Pulfrey, US Navy Waves, Hecla.

I was amazed at the number of women that served their country especially before the Vietnam Era. Military service was difficult and especially so for women. The military was run by "old white guys" who most of the time didn't know what to do with a woman in the service.

Battle of the Bulge:

The following local veterans were involved in the Battle of the Bulge. I wonder if any of them knew each other before enlisting in the military or for that matter, did they even know each participated in the battle when they came home and settled in after the war.

Thomas (Chick) Blair, Don Bowles, Donald "Bud" Craig, Morris Spencer, and Jay Swisher.

US ARMY IN THE 1960s AND EARLY 1970s

Please excuse me while I think back on being in the military in the early 1970s. It is one of those things that we all think about and say, "Glad I did it, not sure I would do it again." How does one find himself in the US Army in the first place? At that time, new inductees into the Army came from one of three sources. Draftee, volunteer, or National Guard. Volunteer may have been a draftee who chose to pick his poison rather than allow the Army to do it for him. Extend his tour of duty from two years to three years and get lucky with a military occupational specialty (MOS) of his choosing or at least a duty assignment that sounds better than South Vietnam. The draftee knew he was going in for only two years and knew he was taking his chances. The national guard guy, the weekend warrior, as we deemed him was only there for basic training and a little advanced training and then back home to attend monthly meetings and stay out of the war in Vietnam. Throughout the 1960s and 1970s, the national guard was not activated to serve in South Vietnam and until the military escapades of the Middle East had not been utilized in combat situations since WWII and Korea. When the president activated the national guard units for the Middle East, all those years of being weekend warriors ended. Shit got real.

I ended up in the Army because I got mad at my mother. Left for college two weeks before my sophomore year began with a chip on my shoulder and not much desire. My grades in my freshmen year were certainly mediocre. Guess the average was C+, and that average was not going to get any better during the first semester of the sophomore year. The drawing for the draft lottery for my age group took place when I was a freshman. My draft number was something like 69, and if Vietnam continued, I was probably going to get that letter welcoming me into the military. At that time, it appeared Vietnam was not going to last forever, so my class was not too worried. Under the new rules, we did not have college deferments, so if our number came up, we were going to go.

I dropped by the Army recruiting office in Sioux Falls one day between beers, and the next thing you know, I had signed up for the delayed entry program (after the semester ended at the end of December 1972) with a guaranteed Military Occupational Specialty (MOS) of 71B. A clerk typist. Sounded like a job that did not involve shooting anyone, or anyone shooting at me, and I was guaranteed at least two years in Germany. Vietnam certainly would be over by then. Didn't everyone want to visit Europe? I had the chance to take a German course in college, but it sounded too difficult.

After three semesters, I was able to generate a GPA of 2.3. I was long gone before my grades showed up at my home address. I didn't have to worry about that "come to Jesus discussion" with my parents after they saw the grades. My dad was an excellent student. My sister was smart, and I was a waste of general family talent. I will admit, however, that I was able to really enjoy that semester of college.

Just before Christmas in 1972, I was trying to figure out how to get from Groton to Sioux Falls to be inducted into the Army. No car. No bus. No parents that had any desire to drop me off. I hotwired a car owned by a friend and drove it through a snowstorm to Sioux Falls. Waved goodbye with $20 in cash and a carton of cigarettes. That is all that remained from a whole summer of work and saving. What else would I need to join the mean green fighting machine? The car thing worked out fine, other than fouled points that required me stop many times to put "heat" into the gas tank and finally getting needed repairs from a car dealer, the trip went fine. What is a little storm and car trouble in the middle of a winter blizzard? As you might expect, not one person questioned why I was driving a car that had been hotwired. Seemed fine to them. I arrived only four or five hours later than expected. Left the car with the owner (he was getting knee surgery) and joined a group of guys who were headed in the same direction as I. Fort Leonard Wood, Missouri, for basic and advanced training. My first jet plane trip.

Most of these guys were just like me. Headed nowhere in life. An assortment of draftees and volunteers like me and couple of national guard guys. Draftees thought we were crazy for volunteering, and we thought the national guard guys were, well, wimps. We thought they were just above the Navy and Air Force enlisted guys. Some of the volunteers were guaranteed duty assignments for Vietnam. Now that is just sad. They were going to be disappointed if the war ended before they had a chance to kill or be killed. An assortment of middle or lower middle—class boys from small town South Dakota.

BASIC TRAINING

Fort Leonard Wood, Missouri, is usually described as the armpit of the US. Hot in the summer and cold in the winter.

Surrounded by little Army towns that had lots of ex-military cab drivers willing and able to meet the needs of military boys. Legal or not. You learn very quickly to wait. Learning to wait is an acquired art but very necessary if one desires to get along in the Army. Did a lot of police call – pick it up. If you cannot pick it up, then paint it. Police that cigarette butt. Strip that cigarette. Lots of problems with controlling the infestation of cigarette butts. Did meet a few guys who were coming back from Vietnam and waiting for discharges. Honestly, not sure I met one that was getting an honorable discharge. These guys were a little screwed up, and it sure seemed to me that I did not need to visit where they were returning from. I remember being in lots of lines. Clothes. Shots. Tests. More tests. Haircuts. That was the strangest. All of us lined up to get our wonderful hair cut off. The clippers had a vacuum cleaner tube attached to suck up all the hair. We walk in with a few quick friends we made and walk out not recognizing anyone. That is the Army. Everyone looks the same, same haircut, same clothes, many of the same dumb ideas.

Basic training if you have ever been involved in high school sports is not really that difficult. If you are in reasonable shape, the physical fitness requirements are not too difficult. Getting yelled at by some guy is easy to put up with and paying attention is not all that difficult. Just getting through the constant cleaning, lack of sleep, playing Boy Scout, sleeping with a rifle, and camping out, is the problem. Forgot to mention that knowing your left from your right is very important. Knowing how to march gives you a step up on many of the guys. Thanks to marching band, I was able to function in the drill groups. Even got to enjoy the long marches, learning the cadences. Did I mention that there were no scientists, MBA students, doctors, lawyers, etc. in this enlistment group? Yes, this was a group of very mediocre people who would never believe that they were the smartest people in the room. Any room. Anywhere. You also meet some very strange guys. This was a time when many of the guys in my basic training company were volunteers but only because the judge ordered it. They would spend a little time with the Army and avoid a little jail time. Even steven. One guy I got to know was a hillbilly who could not figure out what was so wrong with carrying around a sawed-off shotgun under his car seat and pointing it at people who piss him off. Many of these guys with limited education, very limited. More than a few without high school degrees. Honestly, I never knew a person who did not graduate from high school. Until the Army. Lots of drug guys. Driving under the influence was a favorite infraction. Nothing serious, at least as far as I could tell. You end up, in some cases, developing a higher opinion of yourself. You know, the one-eyed man is king in the land of the blind. There were plenty of blind guys in basic training. For information, the typical basic training group was a company (couple of hundred guys) controlled and trained by a cadre of drill sergeants that love to yell, teach, and yell some more. There were company commanders that were captains and an assortment of lieutenants who also liked to teach, yell and train. After a while, it did not surprise anyone that many of these officers had a life span of minutes in combat. Most of the drill instructors had combat experience. The officers, not so much.

I was surprised that the accommodations were a great deal like dorm rooms. Only there were six guys to a room. You got a bed and a locker. You needed nothing more than that. You learned to make a bed and wax floors and generally get along without much sleep. Of course, you also learned to polish stuff. Shoes, boots, belt buckles, etc. You also got to know many people you would otherwise never be associated with in the real world. The company was a mirror of the lower or middle class of the country. Black, white, poor, uneducated, hillbilly, trailer trash, and Hispanic. Most were from small towns with a smattering of big city guys who were lost when it came to marching, firing weapons, or getting along with guys like me.

I will not bore you with many more details of basic training. I am sure that basic training, which is eight weeks long had not changed much over the past 20 years. Little less physical violence from the cadre of enlisted men, I assume, but the same things still happened. Boys were turned into men. Too much beer was drunk on the time off. Yes, people did get abused physically and emotionally. Eliminate as much civilian lifestyle as possible and instill military discipline and move the recruit on to advanced individual training.

Graduation from basic was not exactly an "event." Just marched out someplace, listened to some officer, and then off we went for what they called AIT. I think it stood for advanced individual training but for most of the guys, it was advanced infantry training. The training you get to be an 11B. A grunt. Cannon fodder. Guys who shoot and get shot. Learn to live in tents and spend way too much time outside. Lots and lots of guys were sent to infantry training.

ADVANCED INDIVIDUAL TRAINING

I was promised that I would be a clerk typist and then be stationed in Germany. The first step in this career-defining decision is clerk typist school. You are introduced to a typewriter and lots and lots of Army forms. If you can spell, type and read, it was an easy class. It certainly was for me, and I fulfilled the minimum requirements in about a day and half. Some of the guys spent weeks in this course, either trying to avoid getting a permanent station or because they just did not get it. I was a star in a rather dim room of Army clerk typists. As I was getting ready to leave and waiting on my assignment in Germany, a non-commissioned officer (reminded me later of a used car salesman) came to speak to me about what I should expect in my military career decision. You know the lifestyle of the rich and famous clerk typist. Anyway, he asked where I was headed. Told him Germany to be a clerk typist. He said that was a good choice but, I needed to understand that Germany did not need clerk typists. It did need good truck drivers. Clerk typist might be what I was thinking I was going to be, but truck driver was the more likely the outcome of my career selection. I told him that this was obviously wrong. Army would not lie. I was going to be a clerk typist not a truck driver. I liked heat in the winter. Being in an office. Sleeping in a building. Clean clothes to wear. I had already seen too many truck drivers during basic training, and that job did not look the least bit appealing to me.

The guy was selling something to guys like me. Additional training. Must have gotten a bonus or something to get guys like me to sign up for advanced classes. He gave me a list of classes I could take that would enable me to avoid driving those trucks. I started at the bottom, selecting the classes that took the least amount of time to complete. Such as postal clerk. Two weeks and out. Sorry full. Finance clerk. Three weeks and out. Sorry full. This little exercise in futility goes on until the last class is discussed. It is 16 weeks, a freaking eternity to a guy like me, at Fort Benjamin Harrison in Indiana. It is training for 71C, a stenographer. I had no idea what they did, nor did the guy talking to me. He did say that there would be no truck driving responsibilities and that if I could graduate, I would have a good chance at a great job and assignment. What could go wrong?

Before I leave this, let me tell you a little about AIT. We moved from the familiar confines of the basic training accommodations and "checked" into the AIT Company. Assigned to barracks and given a list of the rules. There were not many rules, just show up for morning roll call, eat when you can, and above all else, attend your classes. My group was a large collection of clerks. Gone were the six-man rooms. Welcome to WWII barracks. Home to 30 or 40 guys. Row after row of bunk beds and lockers. Bathroom had communal showers, what seemed like ten or twelve commodes with no privacy and urinals. What a treat. Not sure I ever used the commodes. Cleaned them of course but would never use them. The barracks were full of all kinds of guys, and it was my first experience with being a minority in such a confined place. Lots of Blacks who ate together, hung out together, and the like. Not much mixing. I will always remember waking up in the middle of the night and discovering one of my 30 roommates decided to relieve himself in the corner of the barracks.

Fort Benjamin Harrison

Not going to bore anyone with the details of AIT stenographer school. Suffice it to say, we were the kings of the clerk typists. Most had college degrees or some college. It was coed with a fair number of WACs (Woman Army Corps) and civilian teachers. All ranks were being educated in this class. Even one airborne sergeant. I guess even guys who jump out of airplanes need a stenographer. All we had to do was go to school every day for eight hours and the rest of the time was ours. No weekend duties. No KP (kitchen patrol). Had our own fast-pitch softball team. Like a real job. They taught us how to type and type fast. We had the best equipment the Army had available to them. Every day was a mental grind. While we were attending school, the Army worked on our security clearances. If anyone failed that little investigation, they were shown the door. Back to being a clerk typist or truck driver. We were being groomed to take care of the needs of the senior Army officers and non-commissioned officers we would be assigned as essentially, secretarial duties. A limited number of spaces were available for our specialties, and we became the top 10% of the top 10%. Many of my classmates ended up at the pentagon and a few in military intelligence. Me, I was guaranteed Germany and was not going to have to drive a truck.

Fort Benjamin Harrison

All we had to do was pass what was called the Goldstein 90 Test. It was a dictation test at 90 words a minute and then a

90-words-a-minute typing test. No spelling errors, no mistakes, all had to be exactly as spoken by Mr. Goldstein. No pass. Sorry back to truck driver school. Was able to pass the test and in fact able to qualify at 120/120. 120 words a minute in shorthand and 120 words a minute in typing. I was one of the best of the best. What an accomplishment. Only problem with this training was that no one ever got around to training the officers or non-commissioned officers to dictate. I never honestly used the shorthand again. At the end of the 16-weeks, I had my Army steno certificate, orders to Germany (V Corps Headquarters in Frankfurt) and a party to attend to commemorate graduation. What could go wrong? Remember your mom told you that nothing good happens after midnight when there is alcohol involved? Let me describe a car full of drunks leaving a club in Indianapolis and driving back to Fort Ben. All goes well getting on post. However, driving in excess of the posted speed, down the road the wrong way, attracted the attention of one of the on-duty military police guys. I was driving. Looking at losing my security clearance, getting busted, and maybe jail. My life was about to change. Truck driving school, here I come. Got pulled over, but the MP was not in the mood to deal with five drunk privates, charge one of them with DUI, and screw up the rest of his evening. He checked to see if anyone else was better able to drive. Found no one in better shape than me. Escorted us back to the barracks and told us to go to bed and not give him any reason to change his mind. There were some happy people who settled in for the short night sleep and a day-long hangover that was coming up. We were about to join the real Army. If there really was such a thing.

V Corps/Frankfurt Germany

When you are assigned to Europe, all solders end up in Frankfurt. The holding area is near the Frankfurt train station, and the Army gives you plenty of time to get used to the time change, figure out where you are going, hoping you don't get into too much trouble screwing around the big city. It should be noted that the holding area was right in the middle of the Frankfurt "red light" district. Prostitution was legal and government-controlled. That area also had many, many bars where the unsuspecting young fellow in green clothing could get some wonderful company from a young lady. All she wanted was champagne cocktails (typically coke or a soft drink of some sort). She would sit on his lap, talk in broken English until his funds were exhausted, and then go on to the next lucky guy. We were warned of such places, but sometimes you just cannot keep a young man from making a mistake. While I never partook in such services, I did get a little tour one night. It reminded me of the South Dakota State Fair and the livestock area. Little rooms with a bed, chest of drawers, and curtains separating each working girl. Pricing was a little over $25 if I remember correctly. However, as far as I remember, there was no touching, kissing, and lots of protection for both parties. Pretty controlled by the government officials. Beyond this location, there were areas like 20 Mark Alley (about $10) where the truckers and soldiers could visit and things were a little less controlled. I found over my time in Germany that many soldiers lived with prostitutes and helped with rent by selling GI cigarettes, liquor, and gasoline. Each soldier could buy five cartons of cigarettes per month along with five quarts of liquor along with gas at the post exchange. The cigarettes were $2 a carton, and the liquor and gas were much less expensive than on the free market. The typical soldier could turn his or her unused items into cash or trade.

I am not sure how long I was there but seems like a week or so. I think the Army had a little problem trying to figure out what to do with me. There were so few slots for the 71C MOS that they attempted to make me a clerk typist again. Since I did not go to 16 weeks of school to be a clerk and drive a truck, I stood firm and told them no. Since I was dealing with other clerk typists, it was not that hard to negotiate. They ended up assigning me to V Corps Headquarters in Frankfurt. I would have to interview with a couple of guys but got what I wanted. I ended up working for the G-1 (general staff) at the I.G. Farben Building.

I.G. Farben Building

I.G. Farben Building in Frankfurt had some history to it. It was one of the only buildings that survived the Frankfurt bombing during WWII. We understand that Eisenhower wanted to have his headquarters in the seven-story building, so everyone was told to avoid destroying it. People said that when the building was first occupied by the Army in 1945, you could see all the way to the Rhein River, about five miles away. Nothing higher than three feet survived the bombs. Hundreds of Germans came to the building every day to beg for food. The building was the largest military building in the world, except for the Pentagon. Farben was a WWII war criminal who abused Jewish and other slave labor during the war, and the rumor was that Jews by the hundreds had been killed when the basements were flooded. Farben employed approximately 300,000 people including slave labor. I. G. Farbenindustrie AG was the fourth largest company in the world at one time. He had his very own war crime trial (sixth of 12). The building went through many name changes over the years. We eventually called it the Abrams Building. Behind the building, there was an officers' club, high school, and other amenities for the military and their families. Just prior to being assigned to the Farben building, the Baader Meinhof gang, a group of revolutionists, bombed the officers' club, killing at least one officer. Same group bombed the officers' club the day after I left and returned to the US some three years later.

V Corps was activated during WWII and was a fixture in Germany during the cold war. It also deployed the first soldiers to the European Theater and assaulted Omaha Beach, Normandy. V Corps fought in the Battle of the Bulge. In 1951, it was assigned to the Seventh Army in Europe along with the 4th infantry Division and 2nd Armored Division. When I got there in 1973, V Corps included the 3rd Armored Division, 8th Infantry Division, the 11th ACR and several other units. One of the V Corps responsibilities was the Fulda Border Gap. That was where it was believed the Russians or East Germany tanks would enter West Germany to start WWIII. It was also assumed that most, if not all, of the Americans stationed in Frankfurt and surrounding areas would be dead in less than a day. The 11th ACR was simply there to slow down what is believed to be 50 tank divisions. In 1973, you could not throw a dead cat without hitting a US soldier or family member stationed in Germany. We were everywhere. Everywhere. Must have been over 250,000 US citizens in the small confines of West Germany. We called the Germans comrades. They called us ugly Americans and would have preferred we find other places to put our ramshackle troops and those runny nose kids and families. They did not like our troops dating their daughters, especially the Black soldiers.

V Corps Headquarters where I was assigned was the administrative headquarters of all the military personnel and their dependents. My section, the G-1, was a giant personnel department for officers assigned to the V Corps units. We also took care of safety issues, race relations, drug programs, and an assortment of ash and trash military stuff. It was headed by a full bird colonel, sergeant major and usually a light colonel and major just to make things interesting. There were probably 75 military personnel assigned to this section, and I was responsible to the colonel and his sergeant major. Personal secretary. You name it, I did it. Need your piano moved, call Private Raines. Tickets for the circus. Call Specialist Raines. You get the picture. It was, however, a great job. No company stuff like KP (German labor did that), no guard duty (MPs did that), no nonsense, just a job. The company commander and his officers and non-commissioned officers ignored those working in the I. G. Farben building. They saw no benefit in getting involved in our business if we stayed out of theirs. They were happy to take care of the cooks, mechanics, military police, etc. Just wanted to ignore the clerks of colonels and sergeants major.

V Corps Headquarters as I said, was in Frankfurt, West Germany. The center of all drug trade in Europe at the time. Hash, heroin, cocaine, pills, etc. Everywhere. A supermarket for the troops and their dependents. I was introduced to hash about 10 minutes after being assigned a room in the barracks. Maybe less than 10 minutes. I did not even unpack before my new roommate introduced me around. Found myself in a two-man room with about 10 white guys in it, all smoking hash. Think of hash as a high-powered marijuana joint. Couple of hits and I tried to throw up out the window. Problem, the window had bars on it. Not a successful introduction to my new clerk friends. Good laugh was had by all. I decided to stick with beer that was available from the vending machines in the hall. So much for my introduction to drugs. Generally, you do not lose a security clearance for beer drinking but sure can with drug use. My security clearance kept me from driving a truck.

Had a successful interview with Sergeant Major (SGM) Haga, Specialist Peterson and Colonel B.D. Wheeler (subsequently replaced by Colonel Sanders A. Cortner). I was hired and went to work. The next day, I had a meeting with the SGM and Specialist Peterson. They told me to get my international driver's license. No problem. Successful. When I got it, they told me to go with Specialist Peterson so that I could learn to drive a two-and-a-half-ton truck. What? Drive a truck. No, this cannot be true, but it was. What could possibly go wrong?

It is difficult to imagine what it is like to drive a two-and-a-half-ton truck with expandable walls around Frankfurt. The truck was very top-heavy with stick shift and trust me, your typical enlisted man was not exactly comfortable driving around. I am not sure anyone ever got comfortable leaving the barracks area with one of those trucks. This city's streets were very narrow and extremely difficult to make your way around. Most drivers parked their cars up on the curbs/sidewalks because there was not enough room to park a car and maintain traffic flow at the same time. It was not unusual for traffic accidents to occur whenever Army vehicles left the confines of the barracks area and moved for military alerts, which occurred frequently. I for one, was really in a sweat every time I jumped in that damn truck to drive. I was given the responsibility of that vehicle until I could pass the responsibility to someone with less rank. Luckily, that was not necessary as the Army made the decision to decommission all of these vehicles and find fixed alternatives when we were out on alerts. They even issued me a jeep so that I was able to transport my officers and senior enlisted men. Much easier to drive and maintain. Almost turned it over entering the Autobahn one day. Scared me and the lieutenant colonel who was giving me directions.

With an international driver's license in hand, I was officially a member of the G-1 office. Some items that might be of interest include:

- Military is big on paperwork. They have a form, report, document, etc. for everything. How else could you keep guys like me busy? Everyone in the office wrote out what was needed and passed it on to me for typing, duplicating, and distributing. The soldier in charge of moving paperwork has lots of power, probably more than the guy writing it up.

- This was all before copy machines. When we wanted copies, we had to get a form filled out, signed by the appropriate approving authority, and the printer would "burn" us copies. Wait in line and waste as much time as possible. Could spend hours doing this.

- Whenever my officers wanted phone calls made, it was usually me who did the calling. I would have to get the other officer's or senior enlisted guy's clerk on the phone. We both played the game. Junior person on first, then I would put them on hold and tell my guy that such and such was on the phone, and he would pick up and the conversation began. Nothing worse than putting on my colonel first when the other side was junior to him. My colonel graduated from West Point in 1953 and had been a colonel for a long time, so he was senior to almost all other colonels. There was a book that we consulted to make sure we knew everyone's date of rank. It also meant that my colonel had been passed over more than a few times for promotion and was just waiting for his 30 years to be up and out he would go.

- Learned very quickly that the most powerful guys in the military were probably the sergeants major. Command sergeants major were like gods. Pity the poor 2nd lieutenant that does not return a salute from one of these guys. Likely to have his first ass burn from an enlisted guy. No one screws with these guys.

- Working day to day was not that much different from a real clerical job. Show up at eight, go home about five or six, and start all over the next day. Day in and day out. Weekends were your own. Living in

Frankfurt afforded you the chance to visit almost all of Europe. Most of us did.

- When I arrived, there were about 50 enlisted guys in our section. Most of them senior enlisted. Very few women (WAC's—Women Army Corps), no Blacks, and initially the lower enlisted men were draftees. This was during the transition from a draft-dominated Army to the volunteer Army. The draftees were serving the last portion of their two-year enlistment, and most were highly educated. I had a year and half of college and had the least education in the section of all lower enlisted men. By the time I left two and a half years later, I was the most educated of the lower enlisted men. The volunteer Army was short of personnel and short on educated enlisted men and women.

- The military was experiencing racial strife like the rest of the country. We had race riots in Germany and lots of issues. Even in our little area, it was easy to see that the Black soldiers were typically in the motor pool, kitchens, drivers, and not likely to be in clerical positions at the headquarters building. When you ate in the dining halls, the Blacks sat together, the Hispanics sat together, and the white guys sat together. I do not remember a Black officer and only one Hispanic lieutenant colonel in charge of race relations.

- There were gays in the military. Always have been. This was back in the time when you did not tell anyone you were gay, and honestly, no one cared. The easiest way out of Germany was to tell your commanding officer that you were gay, and they would quietly usher you out. No fuse whatsoever. During my time in Germany, there was an officer who came out of the closet. He wanted to be gay and stay in the Army. Lots of consternation, but ultimately, he was ushered out and life went on as before. Never did learn if he was gay or not.

- Drugs were everywhere. Except for marijuana. Just could not get it. Lots of heroin, cocaine, hash, and various drug store types of drugs. Mandrax was a favorite among the office guys. I think it was a horse tranquilizer. Whatever your vice may have been when you enlisted, was available in large quantities for you when you became a permanent member of the military. Alcohol was always available, especially in Germany. Beer was an acceptable vice and most of us spent the weekends drinking it. On most street corners, you could purchase a bratwurst, fries, and chase it with a German beer. Once saw a mother and her child waiting for a street car to arrive. Child was having lunch and drinking a beer using a straw. There were no age requirements for the purchase of beer. Even had a vending machine in the barracks that dispensed beer cans instead of soda.

- We were all tested for drugs but usually had to do something stupid to generate such a test. We had drug dogs that frequented the barracks, and every now and then, someone would get busted, then lose their security clearance and start work in the motor pool or kitchen the next day. Senior officers and

- Most of us purchased used cars when we got to Germany. These were beaters that were passed from one enlisted guy to another when owners went back to the states. Cars were cheap. Insurance on the other hand was not; it was very expensive. Most of the time the cars were owned by more than one guy so that we could afford the insurance. A traffic citation could result in a legal issue, so we were all careful. Most of the traffic lights in Frankfurt had cameras and when you ran a red light, you were going to get busted. You just waited until your boss brought it up.

Gibbs Kaserne, Frankfurt

- We all spent more money than we should have on stereo equipment. My room had two other guys living in it, and we had three stereos, an eight-track tape player, reel to reel, 8 or 10 speakers, and lots and lots of records, tapes, and noise. The price of that stuff was low compared to prices in the states. We did have a black and white TV, but since there was nothing but German channels to pick up, it was not of much good. Only late in my enlistment did we get AFN (Armed Forces Network). We did have AFN radio and most of us got used to listening to the old radio shows like Jack Benny.

(Note: the first bullet about non-commissioned enlisted men continues from the previous page: "non-commissioned enlisted men just did not want to screw with anyone who did not follow the rules.")

While stationed with V Corps Headquarters, I was promoted often. From Private First Class to eventually, Specialist 5. Each time I was eligible for promotion, I was promoted. To get along, you had to go along. You also needed a mentor who watched out for you. My mentor was SGM Haga. He had been around the headquarters for about 10 years. As far as I knew, he didn't even want to go back to the

CSM Robert Haga

states. Married to a German lady and had never watched a TV that had more than one English language channel until he transferred back to the states in 1975. He was a scrounger and was able to get just about anything needed. He also had a long memory. You screwed with Haga, he would get you, eventually. He ensured that I was promoted, sat on the promotion board, and recommended me for my Army Commendation Medal. Haga had been in Korea and Vietnam. Highly decorated. However, only saw him once with his dress greens on so that I could see the medals.

My boss was Colonel Sanders A. Cortner. A West Point graduate in 1953. Also, a Korean war veteran and at least did a couple of tours in Vietnam. Also highly decorated. He was good to me and a terror to his subordinates. Spoke to a major I served with some years after our service, and the major always wondered how I could function with Cortner. Cortner scared the hell out of the major. Everyday. Cortner was not able to get his first star because he never got a brigade command so eventually retired. He promised me entrance to West Point if I so desired. When I told Cortner that I was going back to

Col. Sanders Cortner

college and get an accounting degree, he was disappointed but wished me good luck.

After two and a half years in Germany, I was discharged and almost immediately entered the University of South Dakota. I was surprised how much easier it was to study, and either the grades got easier to get or I got smarter. Grades were good, and I was able to get that GPA up to almost 3.0. Since I started at 2.3, I thought it was pretty good. Graduated with an accounting degree, passed the CPA exam on the first try, and went to work with Arthur Andersen & Co., a big accounting firm in Minneapolis. The military did a good job in maturing me, and without it, not sure what would have happened to me. Guess the classmate, who told my mother that I would probably not be too successful and that the Army was the best place for me, was probably very wrong. Very wrong.

I had a good career with Arthur Andersen, staying seven years. After that, I went to work with a client and moved from Minneapolis to Austin, Texas, then back to Minneapolis. Transferred again to Sarasota, Florida, and finally found myself desiring to return to Texas. Came back to Austin and started working for a friend in one of his businesses. Twenty-five years later, still in Austin, and semi-retired. However, I will always think of myself as a South Dakotan born and bred.

Made in the USA
Monee, IL
04 May 2025